With Open Eyes

Experience the Daily Presence of God

Amy M. Bartlett

CHRISTIAN PUBLICATIONS, INC.
CAMP HILL, PENNSYLVANIA

CHRISTIAN PUBLICATIONS, INC.

3825 Hartzdale Drive, Camp Hill, PA 17011
www.christianpublications.com

Faithful, biblical publishing since 1883

With Open Eyes
ISBN: 0-88965-219-8
LOC Control Number: 2003115399
© 2004 by Amy M. Bartlett
All rights reserved
Printed in the United States of America

04   05   06   07   08   5   4   3   2   1

Contents

To Stace,
who sees an unusual Lord
—rugged, perfect, present—
and lovingly shares with me
a camaraderie of insanity
for Jesus.

Special Thanks & Acknowledgements

*C*athy and Tom Wilder, Jennifer and Peter Sander and
Laura and Michael Walker for needing a housesitter at
all the right times during the composition of this manuscript.
The geese and cows and dogs were better editors and inspiration
than you could know, and Gracie and Delta are fine creative
companions. Michael Trent for asking good questions in unusual
ways. You sent me searching for the right words, which worked
their way into this text. Doug Wicks for seeking God's direction
for Christian Publications, Inc., which results in uncanny corre-
lation, making project development a breeze. Gretchen Nesbit
for being an editor who speaks the language of a wordy author
and knows how to round the edges.

Stace Gaddy, the steadfast, unintentional influence behind
my *open eyes*. Coming into my life shortly after the Lord fully did,
his balance of West Texas down-to-earthness and beautiful, understanding intimacy with his Savior infused my own escalating
faith during its most curious and explosive phase. Thank you,
Stace, for your perceptive, passionate, plugged-in spirit and how
it affects your world and me. Thank you for challenging me and
supporting me when I see an extreme God. Your sensibilities
keep me sane, and the nature of your sight keeps me opening my
eyes wider still.

And though there is always reason to acknowledge them, an
amplified thanks to my parents, Chuck and Diane Bartlett,
during this unusual time, for patiently housing me while I read-
just to the West Coast and get over New York, enduring the
ever-present laptop wires, frequent all-nighters and typing during movies, buying me mochas and providing endless material

through their personalities and passing comments. On the day the final edits were finished, each of them affected the project in unique fashions.

My father: When I needed a last-minute confirmation of lyrics and couldn't find them on the Internet, he left his work in his garden and, to my amazement, unearthed a tape of this obscure song from his truck. The tape was broken and warped by spilled coffee and the California heat, but he performed dogged surgery until it not only worked but it reinspired my original passion for this devotional, especially as we sat and listened to it together, picking out voices he recognized from his home church in North Carolina. The song was the seed with which this project began and the perfect place to end.

And my mother: That evening the sky turned an intense shade of pink. With so much to do to close out this book, I didn't even consider that I could take the time to watch that masterpiece. But my mother insisted, as knowing mothers do at just the right times, and convinced me to race to see the sunset, even with deadline looming. I thought I was being either spontaneous or obedient, but when I pulled the car over alongside a field and climbed on top of my car, God's intention came in: I found myself in exceptional prayer and realized how necessary it was to be there with Him before finishing.

Beyond the obvious umbrella of influence they've had on these stories, God used both of my parents that day to tie the final strings together and fluff the bow atop this book.

Introduction

As a child I was given every opportunity to see God . . . and I almost missed Him entirely.

I was raised by two exemplary Christian parents who lived their faith and kept God *real* in our home. They made sure there was always an extended church family behind us, taught me about life by using His Word and generally raised me in the way that I *should* go (see Proverbs 22:6). I saw God at work in our individual lives and in the lives of others who were drawn to our doorstep when crisis hit, knowing, even when they didn't understand quite why, that our home was a sanctuary.

Add to this the phenomenon (it seems a phenomenon to me) that I have always believed in God. Though it took me twenty-three years to figure out the first thing about what that means, and though I'm still learning to act out that faith, I have always known He was there. I recognized my Shepherd.

Yet with all of this as my launching pad, I came very close to missing the fullness of God, because I wasn't *looking*.

After sincerely accepting Christ as a child, I lived the next decade and a half thinking the "Christian thing" was covered. (I respectfully interject here that my parents handed me a much clearer faith than my misinterpretation reveals. But the full discovery of faith depends on one's own path and God's purposeful timing.) I figured I didn't need to weigh "religion" or evaluate God; I'd already explored those issues and found a verdict. What more was there? As for Christianity as a way of life, I would stand up for God in any public arena, no matter how poor an example I was of Him at any given time, and He would be there whenever I had a crisis. That was the main purpose of religion, right? Respecting God as my creator, accepting His salvation, being faithful to Him when He was challenged around me and turning to Him when I was in trouble. I had it all buttoned down.

That was the "faith built on sand" of a troubled nineteen-year-old unexpectedly alone in New York City—the perfect place for a crisis of faith. That's when I expected to see God move. Salvation and crisis: mistakenly assumed to be the two major visiting hours of the Almighty. As I struggled, complained and nearly drowned within the urban tempest, I wondered why He didn't swoop down in His red cape to zap me with strength, righteousness and deliverance. This was His chance to be the image of Him I'd always had—a God who would save me from tough circumstances (perhaps make me strong enough to endure them for a moment) and then deliver me back into the green pastures from whence I came.

I waited for that God for five years, with eyes shut tight. I was blind not only to Him, but to the evil that was trying to undo me. I struggled alone and fought like mad, clueless to the power of the Holy Spirit, but still carried along by a patient mercy. I'd see it all clearly in hindsight, but I spent those years sitting in the palm of His hand, ironically wondering where *on earth* He was.

When He finally caught my face in His hands and began to teach me one-on-one what I was missing, the relief and amazement of His Spirit rushed in with vacuum force. I was shocked by faith. I'd had no idea. All my life I hadn't even known to look for what I'd just found. His Word came to life around me as I encountered His presence in a way I'd never known Him to exist.

So life began—my shocked life of faith. With one peek into the activity of the Holy Spirit, my eyes shot open to wide and amazed. I'm not saying it's been a perfect road since then, but every day attuned to the activity of the Holy Spirit is a waterfall of dialogue, discovery and utter relief. In my new-to-this-life excitement, I celebrated with anyone who claimed this God of Abraham as their own, asking, "Why didn't you tell me it could

be like this?" What I discovered was that no one had told me because they didn't know. People of all different levels of faith,
from nonbelievers to teachers and leaders, were living off of the
spoonful of God they'd been handed by the world, blindfolded
to the banquet, simply unaware that there was more. And then
God prompted me to tell people, through this book, that He is
there, in His fullness, waiting to be found.

To use a phrase you'll find all over this book, "There's *always*
more." To the best of my ability I began to write down the stories of
"more" and of the "possible" that God promises. Whether you read
this book in thirty days or over months or all at once, my hope is that
you walk away with a heightened sense of "devotional thinking":
having eyes that strive to see the constant devotional we live in
Christ. May it spark the light by which you seek to find His Spirit in
absolutely every situation, looking for your "more" from wherever
you stand. From the first Noël, to Calvary, to today, through tears or
uncontained exaltation, in reaping or in hard sowing, the discovery
of Christ as He loves and cares for us in practiced perfection leads to
an undying celebration of His companionship. More than anything,
may He sit and read with you, think and live with you, and open
your eyes to His constant attendance.

I believe there was a reason for my "congested" eyes in troubled times: The night-and-day comparison of life will forever
feed my urgency to share the gospel and my gratitude for this
new world of living in His Spirit. That was part of His plan. But
any day lived without the fullest sense of Him is missing divinity
on earth; it's missing the magic.

So I invite you to read a few of the stories He's knit, through
my life and others'. I invite you to question, grapple, relate, re-
lease, trust, wonder and grow. Everything here is born of true
stories, a sincere heart and a prayer that God would lay it out,
knowing every person who would ever come to read it—His
own personal photo album of memories, testimony and evi-

dence, a collection of images of God in His world, with His children. I don't want to be the one to show you as you flip the pages—let His Spirit show you everything. I only invite you to meet with Him, and to look *With Open Eyes.*

1

That's Him

He who forms the mountains,
  creates the wind,
  and reveals his thoughts to man,
he who turns dawn to darkness,
  and treads the high places of the earth—
  the LORD God Almighty is his name. *(Amos 4:13)*

The heavens declare the glory of God;
  the skies proclaim the work of his hands. *(Psalm 19:1)*

On my first Easter in my hometown in over a decade, the children in my church happened to sing "My Deliverer" by Rich Mullins. It's one of my favorite songs (I have a hundred of them), and it got me, just like it always does.

I sat there slightly overwhelmed by ten years of change. There had been astounding change in the church since I had last been a regular attender. It had grown from meeting in the local Carpenters' Union Hall to a permanent building in its second phase of expansion—but that was expected, foreseeable growth. What I hadn't expected was the degree of change in me. I hadn't known when I left California that God was taking me 3,000 miles away, to "Babylon on the Hudson," to find out who He really was. I had seen an awful lot, I understood

what He had told me so far and now I was home, still with so
much to learn, but ready to go on.

When the chorus began, quiet and slow the first time through, I
could almost sense the entire nation of Israel singing, "My deliverer
is coming; my deliverer is standing by." The haunting, inviting ca-
dence, sung by children who were just babies when I'd left and now
were grown enough to praise Him, painted a strong image of God's
continuing timeline. They echoed again, "My deliverer is coming;
my deliverer is standing by."

Before even realizing what I was doing, I scribbled in the mar-
gin of my bulletin, "*My* deliverer is coming." I stared at those
words and suddenly felt the honor of being a part of a tangible,
ancient and present body—the nation of Israel and my father
Abraham, and this body of believers. The word *believers* is almost
too light to capture the magnitude of the spirit of this group. As
gripping as it is to claim a home in a body of believers that has
been growing within a common faith, recognizing Jesus since the
days when the Word Himself walked among them, there's a
more eternal tie that bonds us as blood relations—through
Christ and beyond Abraham—to God Himself. It adds my voice
to the song that was Jacob's as he wrestled with the angel (see
Genesis 32), or to the Spirit within the Israelites encamped
together by a pillar of fire, who hoped against hope but failed in
the face of promise as humans are wont to do. It's the same
Spirit who drew the wise men across the desert night and stirred
John even in the womb, that "something" that made men believe that Jesus was the Messiah.

A resonation more vast than heaven has been singing since
creation, when the Word was *with* God, "My deliverer is coming;
my deliverer is standing by." I stared at the words I had written
on my bulletin as the rhythm of the song intensified, inspiring, as
intended, the growing knowledge that with every day His return
is one day nearer. Then, as if all of this weren't enough, I found

myself writing just below those words that which is the epitome of peace and perfection *right now*. I wrote, "My deliverer is here."

When September 11, 2001, hit our nation, the question erupted, "Where was God?" It came from every faction, from hurting Christians to hurting agnostics, from the media and the Church, from the left and the right. Everyone adopted the question, and everyone answered according to what was within his own spirit. But it took us a while to realize the difference between the complete infusion of this question into our society after 9-11 and the great lack, the deliberate silencing, of the question that was there only a day, or an hour, before.

Where is God . . . today?

Where was God on September 10? Where was He a month or a year later? More so, where was the question itself, and the questioning, seeking spirit? Where was the freedom of searching for God on public grounds and across the airwaves? Where is the question now? It's an everyday question both for those who believe and for those who do not, both to ask ourselves and to rouse in others. Where is God . . . today?

I was in North Carolina just about a year ago when I heard a well-known gospel song by Bill Burns called "That's Him." It was being sung by a group called Promise, three good friends who have a way of taking on God's voice in remarkable impression. I sat and listened to the distinct sounds of my earthly father's southern heritage, a harmony that sounds like family to me. Add the Holy Spirit and it was home entirely.

I'd heard the song before, but in that moment was struck for the first time by the significance of the lyrics, and, even more simply, of the title: "That's Him." It captures the core of my life, both source and purpose. Everything around me and everything from me is meant to speak the truth of His existence. The lyrics specifically capture the awesomeness of "discovering" that it's Jesus among us, the Savior Himself, the Messiah. The celebration not only of an eternal promise fulfilled, but of The Promise reaching into our lives and circumstances, right before our eyes, and changing everything with just His name. The song dives into the excitement of this with the very first line:

> A tender blade of grass so green,
> crushed in the footprint of the Nazarene
> Springs back and waves a message
> to a bird on the wing: "That's Him!"[1]

What perked my ears immediately was that it was the word *crushed* in this picture that drew the image of praise. It's a persuasive example of looking beyond our human-level interpretation of a situation and looking straight into God's view of it. My pastor said in church just this morning, "If you're looking at your circumstances to determine if God is good, there will be times when it might seem God is *not* good. But if you look beyond your circumstances to God Himself you will always be able to know, and most often see for yourself, how very good He is."

My Deliverer is here.

If we look at the blade of grass, we call it "crushed," connoting "damaged, devalued, lost." But if we look always beyond our proverbial crushed blade, into what it means in relation to God, we find that even our crumpled estate is cause to celebrate, "Jesus is here, Christ is near, walking this world." Our reaction to Him "waves a message" joyously, knowingly, to someone else who might understand, "That's Him." Like the winds that knew He was God and obeyed His whispers (see Luke 8:22-25), our down-to-earth recognition of Him can calm someone else's storm, as a later verse of the song so gently describes:

> He raised His hands above His head,
> saying, "Peace, be still," and the waters fled.
> Then a wave tapped the wind on the shoulder and said,
> "Shhhh. . . . That's Him."[2]

You can expect to find, in time, increasingly less of an asking and more of a knowing—an excitable recognition, a constant reunion as you sense God's hand at work and His love, His character, His voice, His presence unmistakable, undeserved but abundantly around you. You will become aware of the same Creator to which the universe responds in recognition and in praise, the voice that blind eyes recognize as they begin to see, the voice you know deep within you as the same that knit you together in the womb and knew you still before that. Without a doubt and with constant gratitude, discovery and relief, your heart will begin to shout (which can sometimes be done quietly), "That's Him!" In every situation, in trial and in celebration, the question "Where is God?" will be met with a world of revelation as there is nothing left which in its existence doesn't cry, "That's Him." There is no direction we turn that will not testify ultimately of His sovereignty, His reality and His individual love, not a single moment that isn't a chance to reflect all of these things for someone else.

Where is God? He is *here*. Yes, He is "coming again," but our Deliverer is here *now*. Ask your questions, for He has sworn a constant answer for those who seek Him. Look past your circumstances or what you think you see into the face and the goodness of God. Plug in to the Spirit that the winds and waves obey. Then watch and listen as everything in His hands begins to declare, "That's Him. That's Him. That's Him."

Reflections

1. What things in your life have spoken most loudly to you of God's presence? In what ways do you see God's hands working in your life throughout the day? In the lives of those around you? In global circumstances?
2. How can you make sure that the example presented by your life comes to mind when others ask, "Where is God around me?"
3. Ask yourself every day, "Where is God today?" and encourage others to do the same. When you ask this question, do you watch attentively, prepared for Him to answer? And, as He does, in what ways are you able to recognize and tell others, "That's Him"?

Prayer

Lord, I barely know the name by which to call You—my deliverer, my Savior, an almighty creator and Lord who chooses to be both brother and friend. But I know that You are God, the same God of Abraham, and that You are drawing Your people's eyes toward You. Begin with me. Show me more of who You are. Show me where You are at every moment of the day. Teach my spirit the language of recognizing You and fill me with a constant readiness to tell the world through all I say or do—even through just the light in my eyes that shines of You—"God is near. . . . God is here." I know it's You, Lord. I ask You to stay near. Amen.

Notes

1. "That's Him." Words and music by Bill Burns. Copyright © 1991 Chris White Music (admin. by ICG), Hopper Brothers Publishing. All rights reserved. Used by permission.
2. Ibid.

Why Wait?

Each one should use whatever gift he has received to serve others, faithfully administering God's grace in its various forms. (1 Peter 4:10)

Ever notice how we're always promising God what we will do if . . . ? How often do we take the chance to embrace the gifts He's showered us with *now,* to wisely invest the talents in our hands while we're here, starting right where we are?

We're usually pretty good about being grateful for the big things—a healthy family, a lasting marriage, food on the table— and we do our best to live accordingly, serving God in doing good by what He's given us. But experiment with me: When asking for something in prayer, try to identify something with which He's already blessed you that is similar in category to that for which you're asking. Find a degree to which the spirit of your prayer has already been answered and acknowledge that gift with a commitment to serve God in that circumstance, even while you wait on His answer to your original request.

For example, if you're praying for a larger home for your growing family, thank Him for the home you do have and make an extra effort to care for it with the sweat of appreciation. If you're praying for a loved one to find faith, thank God that there is even faith to be found, that He's chosen to put you in that person's life, and actively acknowledge the value of these already-given gifts by making a special effort to do something for them in His image.

In asking one day for a family of my own, I sensed the Lord say, *What about the one you already have?*

"My parents? Not what I meant, Lord."

But the answer continued, *Look at the children I've sent your way for you to hold, teach and love. Look at the sisters I've asked you to listen to, the brothers I enabled you to encourage. Until the day I send your intended covenant family* (if that's His will), *serve gladly the family I have sent you.*

I will claim God with everything that is my life—even before anyone is listening.

I knew what I had heard was right, and I adopted that lesson and purposed to serve my global "family" more ardently, while still praying for one of my own. But the illustration didn't stop there. When I began to make promises regarding what I would do with my own "household" once my prayer was answered, the same response came: *Why wait?* Most of the promises I was making were things I could do already, even with my household of one.

As usual, these lessons snuck in when I wasn't looking, like a surprise party of learning. Some of God's most changing moments come unexpected and unsought. There are answers to prayer that are hard fought for, long asked for and deeply hoped for. But then there are the only-divine intentions, when God settles on the hillside and begins to teach us before we even know we have a need.

One day I took a detour through the Hudson Valley and found myself perched atop a hill, dead-center of a perfect day. I was in a new neighborhood where some houses were still being built. As I watched the residents becoming familiar with their new surroundings, I began to pray for their families and again for my own. (I've been praying for "family" since I was about seven years old, when I dragged a life-sized rag doll around, introducing it as my husband.) As I watched the children spilling across the curves of front yards, I prayed for the chance to make such a haven for my own household, neighbors and friends. I wanted to make a place where God would live and people would come to seek Him.

The prayer spilled out in volumes. "I will live in a manner that tells them of You. . . . I will raise my family to serve You. . . . I will love as You love, Lord, if I have to write it on my rooftop. . . ." Then I scaled it down: "I'll hang a verse on my mailbox. I promise it now."

Days later I found that prayer written in my notebook, and that's when the "Why wait?" struck me. Had I really just told God that I would fulfill a promise of claiming Him only if I got a gift first? *No, I'll start now. A party of one, I'll make my one-room flat a sanctuary.*

The Scripture-on-the-mailbox idea was out, since landlords have rules about things like that, but my front door would work just as well. It didn't matter that I lived on the top floor and only one temperamental man, who rarely ventured outside, would ever see it. Circumstances were not the key, and they never are. They're not even an issue. *I will claim God with everything that is my life—even before anyone is listening.*

Then in a moment of uncharacteristic audacity (approaching the throne boldly, as it says in Hebrews 4:16, has preceded some of the sweetest and most immediate answers to prayer throughout history and in my own life), I added, "*But,* Lord, *You* send me the verse. Let me know that You hear. Encourage me, Lord. Send me Your Word to hang on my threshold."

He didn't even wait a full twenty-four hours. The next day I borrowed an unused lamp from a colleague's office when mine suddenly quit working. It was a cumbersome thing with two bulbs and fat metal poles, but I lugged it into my office, noticing something tinkling under the shade. I plugged the lamp in and settled it on my desk, and when I reached in to turn it on, I found something hanging from the switch. Dangling from an olive-green ribbon was a marble plaque with a Scripture verse engraved on it, and not just any verse. It was Joshua 24:15, and it read, "As for me and my household, we will serve the LORD."

I took the plaque home and hung it squarely in the middle of my door on the same green ribbon and proclaimed, with hammer still in hand, "Lord, where I live, You live. As for me and my household, we—even while it's just me and this party of angels encamped around (see Psalm 34:7)—will serve the Lord. Where I live, You live."

Wherever you are, there is a reason you are there. Your circumstances are not accidental. They are designed with the same precision found in all elements of creation. They are a chosen gift from the Almighty, a handmade assembly not only intended for you, but for the sake of which *you* are intended.

And let's not forget the spiritual principle of "master of little, ruler of much," as found in the parable of the shrewd manager in Luke 16:1-14. Though similar to the parable of the ten talents (see Matthew 25:14-30), the parable of the shrewd manager goes beyond being faithful to what you're given and into the privilege of being trusted: "Whoever can be trusted with very little can also be trusted with much" (Luke 16:10). The idea is more personal. God wants you to do more than simply receive things from Him. Instead of simply showering gifts upon you, He asks you to be trustworthy, now. It's a repeated formula throughout the Bible in which God asks us to be faithful *before* the task itself—before the reward, before the greater need. Will you be faithful with less, faithful before you're fully called to be? Will you be grateful and giving, even with your two little mites (see Mark 12:42, KJV)? Will you trust God's picture of who you are, not as you see yourself or your circumstances but as He sees you through Jesus? Will you look through Christ-colored spectacles, through the eyes of a God who has both read and written the last chapter?

Lord, where I live, You live.

Wherever you are, hand what you have to the Lord and multiply the talents with which He's entrusted you. Open your hand, consider what He has placed within it and start there; start now. Trust Him enough to hand Him all of yourself, just as you are, right where you are, and find a way to live the answered prayer.

Reflections

1. What things do you already have that are similar to things you are praying about? How can you be more faithful in serving God with what He has already given you?

2. Setting aside the imagined final picture of how an answer to a certain prayer will look, are there smaller ways that God has already answered, encouraged or blessed you in that particular prayer?

3. What can you do about your prayer requests to make a show of faith, showing God you believe He will answer them according to His perfect plan?

Prayer

Father, thank You for the glimpses You give me of the future and for Your plans to "prosper . . . and not to harm" (Jeremiah 29:11). But thank You also for what I have squarely in my hands today. Thank You for all that I take for granted, for the beautiful things that I overlook as my eyes are watching the horizon for what will come tomorrow. I know I've missed things so often. Show me how I can be faithful to these things from where I'm standing, how I can serve You with what You have built around me. And for my own heart's sake, let me know also that You hear my prayers and understand my longings with a Father's heart. Your Word says that You do, and I believe it—but if You would, reach to me today and give me a fresh touch of understanding and love. Show me that my desires have reached Your ears . . . and then color my desires with Your will. Take me into Your plan and give me joy in You, right where I stand. Amen.

3

True Humility

Let us therefore come boldly unto the throne of grace, that we may obtain mercy, and find grace to help in time of need. (Hebrews 4:16, KJV)

Dear friends, if our hearts do not condemn us, we have confidence before God and receive from him anything we ask. (1 John 3:21-22)

When I was a few years out of college I spent five months living on a friend's sofa in a tiny Brooklyn Heights apartment. That is not a misprint. Five months in a house with four people, two of them little boys whose cartoons began promptly at 6:00 a.m., in Brooklyn, where the houses are much smaller than in sprawling suburbia. I functioned out of a little box in the dining room where I kept my hairspray and toothpaste. I felt a mix of utter gratitude for the dear family that had opened their home to me and anxiousness to get myself settled somewhere where I wasn't pulling Cheerios out of my bed at night.

I'd already done the subletting circuit, and I'd searched from the western end of Manhattan to Far Rockaway, Brooklyn, always walking away empty-handed. The conversations I had with prospective landlords and roommates sounded more like an urban "worst-case-scenario" handbook than discussions about apartments and leases. A few of my favorites were: the man with dreadlocks who told me it was OK that I was white; he would work around it. Then there was the slick older gentleman who said that he preferred a young female roommate, so I'd be perfect. Or the woman who offered to lower the rent in exchange for occasional babysitting and then told me I should be aware that she'd secured a restraining order against her husband, who'd been known to misuse a gun.

After one day full of such unfavorable options, I headed toward one last potential home. It was a five-story walk-up that wasn't really an apartment, but a plywood setup in the attic of an old Riverside Boulevard brownstone. It had no kitchen, a bathroom shared with two other male tenants and no lock on the mildewed door, and I could have all this for only $800 a month.

I felt like crying but found myself laughing hysterically instead. As I was driving a borrowed car along the West Side Highway, a burst of spiritual audacity spilled out of my mouth. With feeble hands gripping the leather steering wheel of a twenty-year-old Saab, I laughed and jokingly cried, "But Lord, is that really all there is for a child of the King?" At least I thought I was joking, but when I felt a pinch of sincerity in the comment, the lesson became clear.

That was the moment when I began to discover that *true* humility *is* boldness in Him. A large part of fully recognizing God's sovereignty is in allowing Him to be sovereign—recognizing, accepting and embracing the size of our roles in our relationship with Him as He's designed it to be.

I did find a miracle apartment a week later which was to be my blessing for the rest of my Manhattan-bound years, but the lesson wasn't about timing or getting what I wanted, because there's always calculated reason behind His timing and manner of answering prayer. Rather, the lesson—and the joy—came before the material answer to prayer. It came in the discovery of a greater entitlement of faith, a portion I'd thus far entirely failed to see. It is a freedom that is not only for me to enjoy, but which brings joy to the Lord.

It was a great discovery; a liberating gift. It hadn't been my style to be so bold with the Lord, at least not in regards to my desires for myself. My belief in Him was bold, as was my trust in Him to provide for me and for "more than many sparrows" (Matthew 10:31; Luke 12:7). My strength, though, had been in humility, in recognizing God's sovereignty and being glad to bend to it.

But now I began to see a new formula: What is genuinely intended as humility can ultimately be an insult to God's glory, a misunderstanding of His plan, a rejection of His full invitation and perhaps an insult to His love. Sometimes what seems like human audacity—being reverent enough of His sovereignty to adopt a boldness that isn't ours, to say "yes" to the concepts that are hardest to grasp—is actually the truest form of humility.

Is that really all there is for a child of the King?

We make God small by staying within our own set of limitations after He's blasted the boundaries. Don't miss the opportunity to honor the complete version of Him where He, by His existence and through His conquest on the cross, says to come to Him boldly . . . in *His* boldness. Honor Him with asking. Honor Him with your presence. Honor Him by accepting what He's won and promised.

Are you prepared to erase your self-doubt and fears and approach Him without timidity, holding high in your right hand the proclamation that He sent as a simultaneous invitation, command and desperately loving hope that you would respond? *Come to me,* He calls unendingly in every possible way. We find almost as many ways to tell Him no. "No, I don't believe in You." "No, because I don't deserve it." "No, this one's too big to ask." "No,

I'm afraid of losing what I know I'll have to let go of." "No. Just not now, not yet."

Adopting true "fear of the Lord" means shaking off all fear of walking into the throne room. We are called to be sure of His sovereignty and responsive to His description of how He wants us to approach Him, putting aside all that hinders and obstructs us from the obedience of leaning into Him as more than a master—as a friend and a brother.

Of course, as is often the human shortcoming, I promptly forgot the power of the lesson I'd learned—until four years later. He called me again, saying, *Don't shy away. Don't hold back. Talk to Me; yell at Me; hope in Me. Ask Me!*

True humility is boldness in Him.

At the time I was in a place of willing sacrifice, knowing I had to let go of something that I'd tried to make a part of God's plan but which clearly wasn't. I had recently had to let go of almost everything in my life—my job, my town, my miracle apartment with which this whole conversation started—and I was strangling this last little stronghold simply because it was the only tangible future-building tool that remained. But I couldn't ignore God's gentle—and right—guidance, so I did what had to be done to remove that thing from my life. When I had done so, I looked down at my empty hand and it looked . . . empty.

It was one of those deceived moments when I'd momentarily lost sight of the truth, which was that in reality my hand was full and my cup was running over with more than I could hope for. I was crying for the loss of something that was in actuality hurting me, when I should have celebrated with gratitude because God was saving me—again.

But as I sat there, staring at my empty hand, ready for it to be filled aright, I was hit with the invitation to ask "less humbly" than I had before. I was just frustrated enough to give it a shot. Instead of praying in a humble state of asking, I prayed in a bold state of knowing God's sovereignty. I felt myself fighting my misguided weakness, and with a tight fist on the bed beside me, I cried, "No. I am not going to shy away from what You have already authored . . . or authorized." Instead of laying a tearful, doubting plea before Him to fill my hand His way, wondering if He would provide or if the road ahead would be even tougher, I decided to pray as He suggested, boldly believing. I left room, of course, for the knowledge that He might respond in any number of ways. That was left to be seen and wasn't my concern. My job, at that juncture, was to walk boldly into the throne room and lay my heart's desire at His feet. Nothing more, but certainly nothing less.

Keeping this careful balance in mind, I prayed, being sure of His desire to bless His children. I handed Him the boldness He'd called for but which is so hard for me to step into. I set aside my "smallness" for a moment and put on the cloak of His sufficiency as I approached the throne.

In that alone my prayer was answered. The words didn't matter. The request didn't matter. I would have His perfect will—even details beyond my requesting, which only He could know—as long as I remained in Him. The relationship between us was fulfilled in my willingness to learn and accept His boldness, His brotherhood.

A.W. Tozer writes in *That Incredible Christian,*

> God is not satisfied until there exists between Him and His people a relaxed informality that requires no artificial stimulation. The true friend of God may sit in His presence for long periods in silence. Complete trust needs no words of assurance.[1]

Don't take for granted the friendship of a sovereign God, the great intimacy that exists because of the cross. If you're truly "picking up your cross," then reap the full benefit of it. Carry it into His company. Carry it boldly, straight to the throne, because He's called you to come.

Reflections

1. Is there something you shy away from asking the Lord for, something that you think is too big, too difficult, or perhaps too small or insignificant to take to Him? Are you willing to ask Him for it and then leave the results in His hands?
2. Ask Him to reveal to you the full nature of the relationship He's designed for you to have with Him. Then ask Him to help you step into that relationship with confidence.

Prayer

God, teach me the balance between boldness and humility. Wipe away all preconceptions I may have and give me a clear picture of how I should approach the throne. Help me to embrace the liberties that You've already won for me and to realize that You laid down Your life for the treasure of those freedoms, hoping I would live by them. Then, Lord, let me live by them. In my attempts to please You, let me not mistakenly withhold from You the joy of my confiding, leaning and depending on You, my God, my Father. Let me take pride in Your power and Your eagerness to care for me, and let me bring it all, boldly, humbly, to You. Amen.

Note

1. A.W. Tozer, *That Incredible Christian* (Camp Hill, PA: Christian Publications, Inc., 1964), p. 121.

4

The Sky Is Just the Beginning

Each man, as responsible to God, should remain in the situation God called him to. (1 Corinthians 7:24)

I have no idea who I am.

To a certain degree, of course, I do. I know my general tendencies, my personality—which has retained certain elements since birth—my typical strengths and weaknesses. But God's been dragging me back and forth through different careers, cities, identities and "life purposes" for the last few years.

I have believed since childhood, as surely as if I had been reading an assignment sheet, that music would be a key element of my life. My first clear memory of this certainty goes all the way back to when I was only "as big as a tire"—literally. At five years old I was running my hand along the top of a tire of a car in the parking lot of our apartment building, singing "Fish Gotta Swim" from *Showboat* at the top of my lungs. The owner of the car happened to come out and said in a "talking to a child" tone of voice, "Are you going to be a singer when you grow up?" In my "childlike faith," I was confused: I thought that was as clear to everyone else as it was to me.

Leap forward twenty years. I was doing well enough in the entertainment industry, living and working in New York, when circumstances far too detailed to enumerate here moved me abruptly into the literary field. Almost overnight I took on a job as an editor for a New York publishing house and, with a few more pushes from the hand of God, stepped into writing and all that comes with that style of ministry. It wasn't the new field I lamented; it was the back-burnering of music, my deepest passion.

God led me to a conspicuous crossroads and gave me a chance to raise the knife against my beloved, awaited Isaac, a chance to answer a big question: If I had to entirely let go of what I thought would be the art of my life to adopt the craft of His choosing, one in which I found myself less capable, if I had to trust Him with an unfamiliar path, would I? "Of course I would, Lord. I'm not saying it won't be hard at times, but would I? Yes."

*Those are the moments when
His voice is nearly audible.*

In only a couple of months, the "ram" appeared in the thicket and God began to fold the two callings together like a familiar pair of hands (I don't know why I didn't understand from the beginning how well they'd fit). I'd had to learn a new industry, working harder each time I progressed, constantly taking on tasks that weren't "me." Then I worked to meld my new craft together with my old craft, and I was dropped more quickly than expected into imposing positions.

Just as I was finally getting comfortable after a good four years of feeling like a fish out of water, He did it again. I got an early morning phone call inviting me to take on an assignment in yet another arena in which I had barely any experience. It was yet another situation in which my employers had no rational reason to entrust to me that particular task.

By that point, I'd become used to the utterly unexpected in my life, so I was getting better at my reactions, and this time I was barely surprised. No panicking, no tears, no knocking knees (well, at least not too loudly), just an excited remembering of what God was able to do that last time I found myself saying, "You want me to do *what?*" But as I hung up the phone that morning and rolled over and buried my head back into my pillow, I laughed out loud and said to the Lord, "Can't I just once be asked to do something I actually *know* how to do?"

Ah, those are the moments when His voice is nearly audible. *Why?* He answered almost excitedly. *Isn't it so much more divine to do something you* don't *know how to do and to know it's Me at work? Isn't it so much more a joy to trust Me? Watch what I can do; be blessed by the phenomenon and then bless others as you tell them it's Me.* It's awfully true that I'd choose His roller coaster any day over the false confidence and passing comforts of going only as far as I know how to.

We're always in the middle of transition, no matter where we are or how far we've come. We're vessels in the middle of becoming. Consider the pots of the Bible. Yes, the "cracked pots" with whom we can oft identify, but also, literally, the pots that held the water that changed to wine, good wine, at the hand of Jesus (see John 2:1-11). More than a miracle, that wine was an announcement, a revelation in a pot, that Jesus is a miracle-maker. Pots of oil that kept pouring long after they should have been empty were a miracle of might and provision (see 2 Kings 4:1-7). It's become my goal to be a pot, a willing vessel that is available when Jesus is ready to announce His divinity in a new place or multiply the oil within me to burn a lasting light.

It's the full acceptance of "not I but Thee, Lord," which the world may call a weak stance, but which is actually the strongest stance. When we're fighting for control, we're weakening our potential, limiting it to our faculties and, further, making it only about us. Our society is always looking for an edge, a step up, a magic formula. Yet we ignore the biggest "edge" we've got to perfect our lives and make a successful, even eternal, impact on the world around us. Build from His perfect knowledge and His love—or rather, let *Him* build—and it's no longer "the sky's the limit" as the mortal saying goes. Suddenly, the sky is just the beginning.

Don't worry about explaining to people where you're going or what you're doing. Some things are not logical, standard or explainable. You might be asked a million times, "What's the wood for, Noah?" Don't be afraid to tell them, "It's a boat . . . a big one, for all this drought we've been having." Worse, you may have no idea what on earth the wood is for, but trust your task, trust your Potter, your Carpenter, and keep building. When the Holy Spirit is working, we often have to wait to know the full story or the "why" behind what we're doing. It's not our hands at work; thus it's understandable that we might not entirely know what the work is. But it will be amazing when in the end we've done what we could not do, when the rain comes and the boat floats.

God will enable you. He will build you. He will name you, like He named Simon, son of John, when it came time for his new task. Simon became Cephas (Aramaic) or Peter (Greek), identified anew by Jesus Himself as the rock on which He would build His Church (see Matthew 16:18). God was always giving people new names, new identities to match what was to become, things He wanted to tell them about themselves and the purposes of their lives.

I've always known the definition behind my given name, but it was only a year ago that I tearfully realized the depth of it. I received my name by accident. My mother had a million precious names planned for her one and only girl, even "storybook" names like Travis for the air force base where I was born. But against her control she was greatly ill when I was born and other family came in to name me Amy before she could say a word.

I didn't mind. It was my name and therefore I loved it. But recently, as I was preparing to speak to an audience in Colorado, I was paging through notes in which I confessed the one part of God I struggled with most: accepting His love. Oh, I believed in it, because He promises His love, and I *know* His promises. But I didn't understand it. I couldn't grasp it. I couldn't seem to hold it firmly in my heart. No matter how much I believed *Him,* I still shuddered under the confusion of His love. For other people, sure. For me, well . . . I *know* me.

I love being "unidentified" as nothing but His.

This was, of course, just my limited human mind speaking. Deep in the recesses of my heart I was cloaked in His love, but I knew I had a long way to go toward resting in it. As my eyes glanced over those notes, something melted into my realization for the first time in twenty-eight years: My name, Amy, means *beloved.* I'd known the definition all my life, since my grandmothers cross-stitched name-poems or bought me nameplate trinkets at fairs. But now I saw His intention behind the name. He knew what would be my question, my weakness, and He answered it before I was born. He identified me just like he identified Peter, Abraham and Sarah. I was beloved, and He knew I needed to hear it from Him.

I no longer need to know who I am as far as any earthly identity goes. I love being "unidentified" as nothing but His. It's the most enabling identity there is. I can go anywhere, take on any task. There is nothing to frighten me, nothing impossible. I have here "no continuing city" (Hebrews 13:14, KJV), and I can be ready to be faithful to any identity and any purpose.

Come, Lord, name me as You choose, and I will be what You make of me. Who am I? I am thine, Lord, not my own.

I am beloved. That's all I need to know.

Reflections

1. In which of God's promises do you find it most difficult to fully rest?
2. If God called you tomorrow to a large, unfamiliar task, would you be reluctant or ready to take it on? If you were asked to take on the impossible, would you close the door, thinking yourself incapable, or are you prepared to take it on and let God surprise you?

Prayer

Lord, You have described me as Your own child (see Deuteronomy 14:1). It is so hard for a fallible human being to understand the fatherhood of a God like You, but help me to see my identity as You intend it to be. Show me what You saw when You "knit me together in my mother's womb" (Psalm 139:13) and give me the expectant courage to take on whatever You put in my path. Prepare me to respond to Your call by believing that there is nothing You could ever ask me to do that You will not give me the strength or ability to accomplish. Whatever it is, Lord, no matter how foreign or frightening, You take over. You be Lord. Whatever it is, make me willing; then make me able. Amen.

5

Hanging from a Make-Believe Bridge

No temptation has seized you except what is common to man. And God is faithful; he will not let you be tempted beyond what you can bear. But when you are tempted, he will also provide a way out so that you can stand up under it. (1 Corinthians 10:13)

As humans we are most surprised by evil when we truly believe it's something we're not in danger of. We're convinced of our own inherent goodness, and we believe that when it really counted, if given a choice, we would not choose evil and that we would never betray or disown the Lord (see Matthew 26:35). We believe that we would stay awake with Him for an hour in the garden, that we would never forget His promises, even when we're struggling in the desert. But we do, every day.

Just as we pay little attention to the work of God and to the battles of the angels around us (and for us) we are often equally, and more dangerously, unaware of the demons that pursue us. We give them gentle names like weakness, enticement, procrastination, harmless joking, social compromise, playful flirtation. They come to us costumed in the details of our lives as human cries of desire, fear, pain or loneliness. They come as that person, vice, weakness or answer which looks like comfort from where we stand, but which, in the character of sin and Satan, will become a great discomfort if we begin to give in.

We too easily begin to excuse our decisions to sin so they look (to us and others) less like conscious choices of evil, calling them instead unavoidable resignations in battles too hard to fight. "It's who I am." "I don't have the strength anymore." "My circumstances are more difficult and others wouldn't understand."

Picture it this way: It is like we are hanging from a bridge by our fingertips. We know that letting go is a guarantee of certain death (*guarantee* and *certain* are redundant, but purposefully so, for there is no way in which chosen sin is not entirely destructive, to ourselves and to others). "But," we reason, "I'm simply *unable* to hold on any longer to the edge." It's not physically possible to hold on with something as minimally functional as one's fingertips against the weight of one's body. In our extenuating circumstances we argue that our weaknesses, our needs, our hardships are the elements that push us perilously past dangling, into plunging. We reason again, "The wind is pulling at me; the cold is weakening my hands. I'm tired and I cannot hold on. I'm sorry, Lord," and we let go.

There are a million temptations more common to the average person—gossip, lies, lusts, etc.—than the dramatic struggle I am going to relate next, so I hesitate to share it for fear of losing the attention of those who might dismiss the application, thinking their own personal struggles much less severe. Thus I remind you that the following story is a magnified example of the kinds of circumstance that would tempt us to let go of the bridge, but that there is equal danger of the same extreme effects coming from simpler, smaller concessions.

I heard a testimony recently given by a brilliant young woman who had struggled with drug abuse and family problems. She described an evening not too far past when her family was totally

unaware of how completely she was breaking down in her bed-
room, through just a thin layer of wood with a modest doorknob
on either side of it. The outside knob gave no sign of trouble,
while around the inside knob the young woman had wrapped an
implement of death. She was trying to hang herself. She wasn't
just thinking about it, wasn't just battling the inclination; she was
giving in to it. I listened to the sound of her voice as she told her
story, a voice that had almost been silenced but now resonated
through a Times Square ballroom in testament to a present, saving Holy Spirit.

*The hand that holds me, that lifts me
safely aground, is the only thing that is real.*

That young woman had become convinced that letting go of
the bridge, killing herself, was the only way to end her pain, her
ongoing problems with drugs and hatred. Suicide had disguised
itself as freedom, as a good reason to let go of the bridge. And for
a moment she believed it—almost past the point of no return.
But God was in the room shouting louder than the lies, and in
the moment it counted the most, she listened and responded to
Him instead. She didn't know it was Him. She didn't know He
was going to change her life in the days to come. But she responded nonetheless. How close, and how much more prepared
she or anyone would be if we would teach one another to realize
the influence of spiritual lies, to recognize them and debunk
them with His promises.

Even as a believing Christian who has seen God's impossible
formulas proven daily in my own life and in others', I still talk
myself into letting go of the bridge at times. I still let the lies pull

at me. I still believe I feel the cold. Though I see nothing but grievous, brutal sin below me, there are times when I let go so fiercely. I "forget to remember" that the bridge is not real and that the hand that holds me, that lifts me safely aground, is the only thing that *is* real.

The part that makes this human tendency to forget even more frustrating is that the bridge and the river are both planted purposefully. And they are not only planted but disguised, made to look like an answer, an ultimate comfort, a way to stop the tears—the tears which seem, at the time, caused only by having to resist what our hearts want, the tears inspired by the absence of something or someone. When we've cried ourselves to sleep for the thirty-first time in a month, or awakened again only to be hit by the same battle of the heart, it may seem an answer to give up on the battle for the Lord and to "rest" by giving in to the need—which is not need but temptation disguised in a very fragile mirage.

As humans, we are prone to very overt weaknesses. Know it; accept it; prepare for it.

It's a temporary insanity, like Esau giving up his birthright because he was influenced by hunger (see Genesis 25:29-34), or a drug addict who literally sells his child for a fix. It is amazing the things a human being will agree to or fall for after prolonged exposure to pain, fear or any threatening existence, like the insolence of wanting to die after years of an agonizing illness. Just as deceptively, how easy it is to welcome sin when it *seems* like it will ease our unremitting heartache—a heartache which, also only seemingly, comes from resisting whatever our current temptation might be.

As humans, we are prone to very overt weaknesses. Know it; accept it; prepare for it. How? By admitting this weakness and pursuing the God who is overt and final Strength. Pay attention, for yourself and for others. Know when Satan has deceived you. It's shouted all over the Scriptures and, by God's Spirit, into your life. Trust Him to reveal the truth to you and live for it. Plug into the spiritual happenings around you, realizing that more is going on than you're aware of—good and bad—always.

You need only to look at Jesus' temptation in the wilderness to recognize the power and worth of resistance, the importance of hard-won choice, the formula of faith. If you were not tempted, if God consistently looked like the easiest, most satisfying choice, then your choosing Him might be nothing but self-gratification. But will you choose Him if for a moment you don't want to? Will you choose Him just because He's right? Will you fight for Him? Will you be faithful?

So many people have lost so much that they loved because they thought they wanted something else. They walked into the mirage only to be greeted by something so much worse in the reality of good versus evil. Their loss is doubled in the heartache of knowing what would have been sustained if they'd only held fast to God's promise to pull them through. We must remember that everything which seems to point us away from resisting temptation or makes faith difficult is a mirage. Get through to the "morning," the daylight, and the Truth will soon become evident again.

It says in Scripture, "Resist the devil, and he will flee from you" (James 4:7). My mistake was in thinking this meant I only had to resist once, that I could boldly say "no" in the face of temptation and would suddenly be strong and unbothered again. But no, the devil flees and returns with many more (see Matthew 12:44-45). So continue to resist. God's promises are not in vain.

It may take forty days in the desert, or longer still in a flood of tears, but truth is truth and this temptation, too, shall pass.

But prepare to face the same temptation again at any time. Remember the strength of God to deliver you and cling ferociously to that strength, to Him. "Things" are never what they seem, including God at times, when you think He's not enough, not near, not patient still. Things are never what they seem, but they are always what He promised they would be. Ask for His eyes to see the difference between light and darkness. Ask to see and believe the bigger picture in your heart *now* so evil will be powerless to deceive you. Know that you'll have to ask Him again, every time. Be ready.

You may have to repeat this roller coaster cycle more than once, but remember that you are not relying on your own fingers to hold you to the edge of the bridge, in the cold and the wind. As a matter of fact, there is no bridge at all. The *threat* is real. Its destructive ability and nature are not to be trivialized. But the ultimate sword of death and ruin is met by the double-edged sword of mercy, which eliminates the threat and turns gently upon you to perform a delicate and healing surgery.

You will defeat huge temptations, generational plagues, and you will lay down a new highway. You will find yourself standing firm atop the bridge, experiencing a million different sensations of victory. It's been defeated—the one temptation that has beleaguered you your whole life, the one that has broken you before and helped you to trouble others. It was another chance to fall, to shatter on the rocks below, but you are not there, and those rocks don't know you. You and yours are safe atop the bridge, and you have seen the strength of God. You will know of it firsthand the next time, and you can shout it from the roadway so that others may see and know God's delivering power.

If you have been there, hanging, and know how both choices end—the letting go *and* the holding on—then please, tell others what the Lord can do, what He *has* done (1 Chronicles 16:8). Tell them of the skilled deceits of evil. Help them through their forty nights. *And forgive them.* We have all been lied to in different ways by a personality of evil.

As much as God is a "person" with intents and plans, so is Satan, who, as long as we're still here on earth, is "roaming through the earth" (Job 1:7) and "looking for someone to devour" (1 Peter 5:8). He knows the gates least guarded in our hearts, the chinks in our armor, and he brings his forces in through the back doors, the weak doors. Don't give Satan credit for any power; you have an almighty Victor who is constantly fighting for you, with a guarantee of triumph if you ask for it. But be aware of every gate. Put the God of Abraham at them. His angels are stationed for your sake. As much as you see your temptations, see His hand more. There is nothing more powerful done in your name than what is done by the One who watches Israel, who is watching you. He has won even this battle.

Reflections

1. Can you remember a time in your past when you knew you were making a mistake, but let go of God anyway?
2. What weaknesses, fears or vulnerabilities do you have that need to be strengthened now in order for you to avoid falling to that temptation should you face it again in the future?

Prayer

Lord, see me when I cannot see through to Your truth. I am on this earth where Satan's lies can blind, and I admit to You that it's often my own actions and small decisions that open the doors to those lies. But Your truth is stronger still, and Your truth is what I want, Lord, what I choose.

Watch me carefully and protect me, but awaken me too, and don't let me go back to the same faults over and over again. Don't let go of me when I am weak and letting go of You. Forgive me, Father, for the compromises, for my repeated faithlessness, for the times when I walk knowingly out of Your hands. Even then, I know You're Lord. Give me a way to use my past failings to lead others closer to You. And though it's far from what I deserve, let me know what it feels like to be set free. Amen.

6

The Twelve-Dollar Gospel

For your Father knows what you need before you ask him. (Matthew 6:8)

Before they call I will answer;
  while they are still speaking I will hear. (Isaiah 65:24)

There are many heart-melting illustrations of how personally God cares for each of us, but there's one fatherly trait that I find particularly endearing and terribly humbling. It's the fact that the Almighty God, creator of the universe, maker of the stars, ruler of the heavens, is not the least bit fazed by our blunders, but rather anticipates them, makes room for them and commands His angels accordingly, knowing the missteps will emerge like clockwork. It becomes almost amusing when we spill the proverbial glass of milk and realize He's already sitting there with sponge in hand, waiting. How embarrassing—but how patient and loving is the God with the sponge.

I got a good reminder of God's eternal provision from an unexpected, contemporary source. He sewed a parable out of the elements of my day, just like He's been doing for people for mil-

lennia. It's a parable of finding God on the sidewalk, of a Metrocard through which God assured me that He knows where He's
taking me, how best to get me there and that He has even accounted for the mistakes I will surely make along the way.

I was changing jobs, making the transition from one company's
pay calendar to another, which can leave a person hanging a bit fi-
nancially. My first payday on the new job was only five days away,
though, so I knew I'd be fine after that. I just had to do a little math
and figure out what I would need to get along until then. It wasn't
much. There were plenty of groceries in the fridge, and I didn't have
any personal needs so pressing that they couldn't wait a few days. All
I would really need was enough to pay for transportation.

But my bank balance was dangerously low. The next day was
the last day on my unlimited monthly Metrocard, so I would
have to squeeze as much of my transportation needs as possible
into that day since it was already paid for. Did I have enough
money to pay for the subway until Thursday?

I was still calculating in my head, counting and walking, bal-
ancing figures on the ledger of a sidewalk passing underfoot,
when I came "toe-to-toe" with a little yellow Metrocard lying
face-up in my path. I was barely surprised. I think I laughed out
loud in recognition of provision. I even caught myself looking
over my shoulder, expecting a snickering angel behind the bend,
like a kid with a surprise, waiting and watching animatedly to
catch my discovery.

I picked up the card and threw it in my bag with the intention
of running it through a reader the next day to see if it held any
value. I must point out, for the out-of-towners, the unlikelihood
of the circumstances. One sees plenty of empty, discarded
Metrocards lying about at subway stations, but finding one in the
middle of the sidewalk on Seventy-fifth Street. . . . It wasn't un-
heard of, but it was peculiar enough to suggest the hand of God
at a moment of need, such as it was.

The next day was Sunday, the ever-busy "day of rest," and in my rush to climb on a waiting train, I'd forgotten I had two Metrocards in my bag. I pulled out the first one my fingers touched and ran it through the turnstile.

I knew immediately what I had done when an unfamiliar message popped up on the screen. There I was, dead in my tracks, Metrocard poised in great error, an "oh no" visage frozen on my face. Not only had I now wasted the last fare that could have gone on my unlimited card, but if there was any value on this "gift" card, I had wasted one of those fares as well.

He sewed a parable out of the elements of my day.

But wait—the screen had a dollar amount on it. Even if I *had* wasted a fare, I was missing the fact that this card was surprisingly not empty. I took a closer look. The screen read $10.50. Not bad for found money, and that's after subtracting the fare I'd just scrapped. That's when the full weight of God's perfect provision hit me.

I was still standing in the turnstile having a silent, one-woman Bible study trying to put the pieces together when I realized just how perfectly they fit. Let's do a little math: Each fare is $1.50, one way. I'd just used one, so the original value of the card had been $12.00, and I now was left with $10.50. I needed one round-trip fare for each day, Monday through Wednesday—that's $3.00 a day, for a total of $9.00—plus a one-way fare for Thursday morning, just enough to get me to work to pick up my paycheck. That would be an extra $1.50. Add that to our $9.00 sum from before and we have $10.50. The amount on the card: exactly $10.50. God not only knew my needs to the penny; He provided over and above to cover the mistake He already knew I'd make.

Does God always send us money on the sidewalk? No, not every time. Does it mean when He doesn't that He isn't concerned with our need? Not at all. He's always concerned and will provide as He knows best. But this wasn't about money or my morning commute. It was about a God who knows, cares and provides for a need even greater than what's lifted in prayer, knowing the number of hairs on our heads (see Luke 12:7), the number of pennies *not* in our wallets, the mistakes that we will make.

> He's already sitting there with
> sponge in hand, waiting.

He has done the same with our sins. He provides beyond them. Have you ever fallen into a sizable sin immediately after He's showered you with blessing? I've done this myself and fallen prey to thinking that by doing so I would lose a measure of His love. I get lost in lamenting, "He has just shown how much He loves me, and barely a moment has passed before I returned His grace for sin." But there's a great difference between repentance and self-condemnation.

Let me remind you that *as* He was sending the blessing He knew the sin you would commit the very next day, or the next hour or the next moment. The love you felt from Him before you slipped is the same even in the midst and aftermath of sin. As He shouldered the cross, your sins *happened*. He knew then of sins you haven't even encountered yet. He knew, He loved you as you were and He paid for them all.

God knows the heart of man. He knows about the presence of sin within it, yet He loves that individual soul so much that He provided Jesus to become salvation. Jesus was perfect, but it was when He encountered our imperfection that the gift became perfect as well. All that is left is for us to accept that gift.

His is the final victory—without contest and unchanged by our mistakes. He's got tomorrow covered in every way. Not only is the lily dressed finely and the sparrow closely watched and the hair counted as it falls down the shower drain, but He also knows our mistakes and sins in advance and has already accounted for them—all of them. He provided not just $10.50, but all $12.00. His name is Jesus.

Reflections

1. Do you find yourself worrying about making a wrong decision or taking a wrong turn?
2. Do you believe God is able to lead you safely into His plan, no matter what?
3. What can you let go of right now to accept that He knows where He's taking you, knows how best to get you there and has accounted for the mistakes you will make along the way?

Prayer

Lord, help me not to worry, understanding that worry is a form of doubting You. I know that I will make mistakes along the way, grand and small. I know I'm human and it's my nature be imperfect. But, when I take a wrong turn, help me ahead of time to trust and to know that You've provided perfectly, already knowing the details of my anticipated shortcomings. I invite You in to be Lord, to love me as I am, and I will enjoy the fact that You know what it will take to get me where You want me to be. I ask only that You hone my eyes so I can see the provision when it's there—even on the sidewalk—and then acknowledge that it's You. My imperfection is only an open door for Your handiwork in my life. Thank You for Your angels, and thank You for sending them to me so creatively. Amen.

7

Beyond the Curtain

Call to me and I will answer you and tell you great and unsearchable things you do not know. (Jeremiah 33:3)

Therefore, brothers, since we have confidence to enter the Most Holy Place by the blood of Jesus, by a new and living way opened for us through the curtain, that is, his body, and since we have a great priest over the house of God, let us draw near to God with a sincere heart in full assurance of faith, having our hearts sprinkled to cleanse us from a guilty conscience and having our bodies washed with pure water. (Hebrews 10:19-22)

It wasn't just a low point. It was the lowest point in my entire life thus far. I finally understood the term *depressed*. Though I was normally someone who was more the "eternal optimist," even occasionally labeled a "Pollyanna," I was deeply grieved. When I finally reached that juncture where every day from dawn to dusk was being spent in tears, I knew something had to change. I was at the point of sorrow where you either change or die.

I had just gone to the corner store for a bar of soap (the "cleansing" significance of which I hadn't realized until telling this story again just recently). Tears pouring down my cheeks, I

was alone in a questionable section of Brooklyn, which had become my neighborhood just after college. My family was 3,000
miles away, most of my friends had moved after graduation (I
stayed to take on Manhattan) and I didn't even have a church
family. When I got to the corner store, I dried my eyes and took
a deep breath. The clerks behind the counter knew me, and I
didn't want any questions.

I bought my little blue-and-white-wrapped bar of soap and
took my plastic bag from the counter. The minute my foot
touched that first inch of gray speckled cement, one step outside
of the store, the sobs started again, uncontrollable, and I'd had
it. "I can't live like this!" I cried to the Lord, fighting with Him as
I walked the half block back to my $245-a-month room. "Lord,
when people tell their stories of hitting a point like this, it's always just before finding You. If I have You already (I'd believed
in Him all my life), then what's left for me to find? What hope of
change is there for me? What else could I possibly need—or
what can fix this—if I already have You?"

By the time I got back up to my apartment, He was finally
ready. Or, I suppose, *I* was finally ready after years of struggle,
and He knew that. He whispered the most obvious thing to my
heart: *Yes, you have always had Me. But I have never once, from the beginning, had you.*

It was true. I'd been given every proper chance to know Him.
I was raised by phenomenal parents. I'd had a strong church
family back home and a good life in general. But somewhere long
ago, I'd stamped "Christian" on my life papers and stopped
there. I didn't look further, didn't even really know that I should.
Even if I had wondered about God now and then, I didn't know
the volume of what there was to be found. I had no idea what life
would become from that moment on.

The change in me only began at that moment. "New life" has
arrived in my heart time and time again through the years. There

in the beginning, when I thought I'd lived my whole life in the fullness of Christ, I really had only His salvation. I was deaf to His voice, which had been calling me to draw nearer to Him for so many years. He had been calling to me, knowing the day that I would finally respond. I was living at times in a virtual hell when not only could I have been free from it, but I could have been here in a day like this, where He is active and evident, where His presence often overwhelms me to tears, where His purposes steer me toward greater designs than I could have ever considered, much less aimed for. When I prayed back then, I didn't know to ask for those things. I don't ever want to go back.

"Yes, you have always had Me. But I have never once, from the beginning, had you."

If I had known, perhaps I could have saved myself much time and heartache. (For the record, though, I know that God had a purpose in the hard times as well, that there may have been a purposeful blinding of my heart's eyes for the sake of a fuller understanding when the time was right. Sometimes God creates a vacuum so that He can rush in with greater force and volume. His timing always has purpose.) Now I *know* how it feels to be in the dark, how it is that people can be in some of the life positions they're in, and that knowledge fuels me to their sides. It's why I run with the gospel in my hand. I'm looking for those who are where I was and beyond, perhaps wondering, as I did, why no one came to tell them that there is more to God than they know.

I tell you, don't miss out when your rescuer is standing ready. Don't miss out even if you think you're already on solid ground. No matter where you are on your journey through this world,

there is a surprise waiting for you, a greater world, a greater existence of God, a new way of living.

If you don't believe in God, the search to find Him is much
more simple and sure than the world would have you think. Ask
Him to reveal Himself to you. It's impossible for Him not to answer a sincere heart. He promises, "Seek and you will find"
(Matthew 7:7).

If you *do* believe in God, ask yourself if you believe in His
presence and power enough to change what you think is permanent or impossible. Ask yourself whether, even when certain
things stir up fears or sorrows, you have an ultimate rest in Him,
a gut calm, even in the midst of tears, that is satisfaction. If
you've received new life, then ask Him for the next step of trust,
the nearer hold of Him. Ask Him to open His hand, to pull back
the curtain and let you live in His fullness, not missing *anything* of
Him.

There is always more of Him.

If you are already living moment by moment in His Holy
Spirit, do you consider it such a gift that you don't imagine there
could be more of Him and have ceased expecting more? There is
always more of Him. Even when you have a solid relationship
with God, don't get so comfortable that you forget to seek Him
further and trust Him with greater calms, greater risks and
greater confidences.

Until you stand with Him in person, there is more of Him for
you to discover. God is always ready to pull you nearer, higher
out of the treacherous canyons; He is always there with a new
idea for you. Without fail, every time I think I've found the fullness of life as He gives it and am ready to settle into "honing" it, I

notice a pinpoint of light shining through a paper-thin wall, hinting that there might be more. Get into the habit of understanding that there's always more.

When Christ died on the cross, the temple curtain, several handbreadths thick, tore from top to bottom. God does nothing without an incontestable truth and message within it, so don't overlook the loud announcement there in the supernatural hand of God on earth. The hands that threw the stars into the sky grabbed a piece of woven fabric more than a foot thick, a curtain whose design He'd decreed far before in the Old Testament, and severed it in two to affirm that there was now no separation between God and man. From the moment "it was finished" on the cross (see John 19:30), God made it so that anyone, through Jesus, can *belong* in the holy of holies with the Spirit of God Most High, Ha Shem, the unspeakable Yahweh. There is victory written in the letters of your name. Don't waste it.

I promise you, because He has promised it, that no matter where you are, there is more of God, a life-changing degree of "more," to be found right where you're standing. Don't hesitate to walk into the holy of holies and discover what has before been hidden. Ask Him for whatever is next. Ask Him to take you beyond the curtain.

Reflections

1. Are you prepared to ask for more of God and to receive what He will bring?
2. Ask Him for a greater measure of whatever it is He wants to reveal of Himself: love, wisdom, patience, His Spirit, etc.
3. Ask Him to reveal to you the next step in knowing Him.

Prayer

Lord, I'm ready to know You more. If all it takes is to ask You, then I ask. Pull me in closer and take me to the next level. Show me pieces of this relationship I could never know to ask for on my own. I want the supernatural in my life. I want the degree of life that You've made available to us, but by which we so rarely attempt to live. I want more of You. I pray for this world as a whole, that we may globally see more of You, more of Your hand at work, more of Your Spirit recognized and praised. And I pray for individual lives, for whoever is looking for You today, wanting more but perhaps not knowing to ask, or at least not knowing how. Don't let them live another day apart from the refuge of Your Spirit. Speak loudly enough to get through to them—and to me—for whatever comes next. Take me there, beyond the curtain, and in Your presence let me live. Amen.

8

A Silent and Gentle Rain

As the rain and the snow
  come down from heaven,
and do not return to it
  without watering the earth
and making it bud and flourish . . .
so is my word that goes out from my mouth. (Isaiah 55:10-11)

I was profoundly moved just now by something very simple, something I'd never before witnessed in exactly this manner. I'm seated on a high deck overlooking a very large creek—a river by my "I've lived in New York City for the last ten years" standards. As I paused in my writing, I noticed a few small centrifugal circles in the middle of the water, which I assumed were caused by fish beneath the surface. But then there were more and more circles. A very, very large school of fish? The circles began to pockmark the entire face of the water, clear across to the opposite shore and left to right around both bends of the creek.

It was rain—such a silent and gentle rain that I had no evidence of it from where I was sitting tucked far under the eaves. There was no sound, no teetering leaves, no chill, not even enough size in the raindrops to wet the edge of the deck. All of those things would soon follow, but for the first minute or two there was nothing to prove the rain's existence except the water stirring water at the bottom of the hill. A thousand drops of rain changed the view. No question, the rain had come.

The rain was dramatic in its quietness, in its understatement and its lack of other evidence, and it reminded me of all the ways we'll never know how the Spirit of God has multiplied through our lives and into others. The sweet stories of lives and paths that have been changed by a timely word or an anonymous action could fill a library. The most remarkable of them are usually about the gospel itself, about Jesus coming into someone's life, but there are other stories too: the card that arrived at just the right time, the call that came at a pivotal moment, someone with the guts to say "Jesus" or simply reach out in love, changing the course of a life and perhaps even the course of history.

The rain on the water had changed the manner of all nature around it.

One of my favorite stories comes out of Pacific Garden Mission (PGM) in Chicago, where thousands of similar stories take place (God is particularly busy on that corner of State Street). This one dates back to the early 1900s when Mel Trotter—who referred to his estate at that time as "an everyday, every-hour drunk"—was headed to Lake Michigan with intentions of suicide. After a ten-day drinking binge, he'd returned home to a traumatized wife who told him their infant son had died and she had been unable to find him to tell him. Halfway to the lake Mel was stopped by, as he describes it, "a friendly face, reaching out." He had encountered the doorman to the mission, who had been there with love to stop the darkness in Mel's life. Mel Trotter not only found love and the Lord when he walked through the doors of PGM; he found the rest of his life, as he later took on the task of running the mission and opening sixty-seven other rescue missions across the country. Preaching from coast to coast, he was soon nicknamed "the happiest man in the world, the man who raves about Jesus."

Another well-known story is the one often shared by Dr. Fred Craddock about a young boy named Ben Hooper. Shunned and ridiculed by his small town, Ben's only crime was in being born out of wedlock. He hid from the public most of the time, staying home, fearing school, sitting in the back row at church so he could duck out quickly and avoid being seen. But when Ben was twelve years old a new preacher came to the church, and on one particular Sunday, Ben got caught in the exiting congregation. The new pastor stopped him and asked the question Ben daily dreaded, "Son, who's your daddy? Whose son are you?" The crushing weight of embarrassment and frustration was about to settle in when the preacher, who had quickly translated the reactions of those around him, continued with a smile, "Wait a minute, I know who you are. I see the family resemblance. You are a child of God." It was that one simple message, added to the preacher's final declaration, "Boy, you've got a great inheritance. Go and claim it," that changed the path of an entire life. Ben Hooper went on to become the governor of Tennessee.

In another story, Corrie ten Boom illustrates the importance of leaving things to the Lord when she tells of sharing the gospel with an intoxicated man who was lingering in a hotel room after a party. Feeling like every word from her heart had missed its target, she left the room deflated. It wasn't until she shared the story years later, poking fun at herself for getting mired up in her own agenda, feeling cocksure of "evangelism" and losing sight of the more precise concerns of God's Spirit, that a man came forward to tell her the *real* end of the story. He had been another of the inebriated partygoers and was passed out under the bed in that hotel room. He woke to overhear her sharing with the other man the love of Jesus and the "no matter where you are" nature of the gospel. He was forever changed, crying beneath the bed, and no one in the room was the wiser until the whole story was told years later.

Appropriate to this image is one of my favorite Bible verses, my favorite part of it being the God-sized vow within:

> As the rain and the snow
>   come down from heaven,
> and do not return to it
>   without watering the earth
> and making it bud and flourish,
>   so that it yields seed for the sower
>   and bread for the eater,
> so is my word that goes out from my mouth:
>   It will not return to me empty,
> but will accomplish what I desire
>   and achieve the purpose for which I sent it.
> (Isaiah 55:10-11)

The rain on the water changed more than my view. It changed the manner of all nature around it. Before the rain had become noticeable, geese tottered in off the water, mourning doves began to land on the telephone wires and the horses left the neighbor's pasture with a comical *harumph*. Now I sit in a sun-drenched downpour, curtains of rain catching the light like stars and falling from the eaves around me. It's a breathtaking thing to see the full development of what was promised by a tiny ripple on the river. But should we never see the results of our ripples, we can trust God with them. He vows that His Word never returns empty but always achieves the purpose for which it was sent, *always* accomplishes His desire.

There is so much the Holy Spirit can do when we simply live His love and love the gospel. As a baby learns from what he feels and sees before he is old enough to understand language, the effects of what you do in the love of Christ are felt before you can consciously see the hand of God at work.

Trust that what you do that is unseen (see Matthew 6:1-6) will be used by Him both for your sake and for others. Trust that there are reasons that He asks you to take certain leaps of faith. Trust the importance of making the small but right decisions and choosing the kind word, the honest intention and the way you know He would want you to take, even when it's hard. He'll set the miracles in motion, and occasionally He'll even let you see the rain—every gorgeous raindrop that falls, every life that's been lifted, helped or changed. You'll see the fuller circle, His grander intentions.

He'll set the miracles in motion, and occasionally He'll even let you see the rain.

There, to my left, just over the pine, is the rainbow. You had to know it was coming.

I promise you, there is no good gift He doesn't use. There is no wasted effort of love. Believe the weight of it, and of His unchanging character, of His love for *everyone,* and put it into motion. Actively, decisively, love one another and watch what He will do.

Reflections

1. In what silent ways might it be evident to those around you that Jesus is Lord of your life?

2. What simple touches can you bring to someone's life that would tell him or her that Jesus is near? In what ways can you be the "gentle rain" in that person's life?

3. What small decisions have you made that ended up having a larger impact than you expected? Are you facing choices now that could multiply into a greater good in the future?

Prayer

Lord, I will never be able to see the full effects of what Your Spirit is able to accomplish in what was begun in love, but You've promised that the rain never comes back without first watering the earth (see Isaiah 55:10). Lord, rain on me, reign in me and fill all that is dry. Bring to life all who are parched. Inspire me to reach out in Your name, sometimes simply with a quiet presence, but always alive with Your intention. Let me see the beauty of Your hand and long for You in everything. Whatever of this world You hand me, let me return it tenderly to Your loving hands. And, whenever You will, let me see the rain. Let me live in the light of the rainbow, that my life may be drenched in the color of Your care and in the joy of Your promises. Amen.

9

Not My Feet

"I have swept away your offenses like a cloud,
    your sins like the morning mist.
Return to me,
    for I have redeemed you." (Isaiah 44:22)

*L*ife is not fair. I know of a woman who lost two children to drunk drivers over a decade apart. I know of a well-known Christian personality whose father left one day without a word, shortly after which both of her siblings died of separate causes. Still another woman lost three of her children on the same day, each to unrelated accidents. Though these examples are similar in category, they're just a feeble reference to a fact that we all know: Life is full of things that are simply unfair. Calvary is one of them.

I have often asked God how Christ, the gift of salvation and grace, can stand with no condemnation in His heart when the face that, in heaven, was too glorious to comprehend is now daily spat upon and accused by us. We, the only ones who are due accusation, debase the Innocent who came not to condemn but to save (see John 3:17). I get so blood-boiled even when someone yells at me on the freeway for something I didn't do wrong, and even more so in serious situations of injustice, when I see the innocent wrongly accused and the overzealous gathering to condemn without knowledge. "How," I often ask the Lord, "could You, in all Your knowledge, not cry out the truth? How could you not silence the crowd with Your simple holiness?" We're going to attempt to answer that question in a few pages, but for now we'll just focus on the "questioning" itself.

There was a period in my life when I struggled with accepting God's grace simply because I didn't think it was "right," as in "fair" (which it's not). In my sometimes self-destructive way of being "true to the moment," there was a time when I shied from grace because I couldn't come to terms with receiving it; it wasn't "right" to take it, if I were entirely honest and fair.

Life is full of things that are simply unfair. Calvary is one of them.

One of Satan's most precise attacks is in convincing us to cut ourselves off from God's grace because we perceive that something, somewhere, isn't "fair" or suitable to our limited comprehension. Such a mind-set, while it would seem one of humility and meekness, actually has us claiming that we're bigger than God and far more wise. If He says that we are "redeemed" and it is done, and if it's the wish and cry of His heart to hold us, then refusing that gift is not the more humble thing to do. It's the more cruel thing—both to Him and to ourselves—and certainly the more unfair, because everything has already been done and paid for. It would be such a waste to refuse God's already-given love.

My mother always says, "Don't take someone's blessing away," referring to the hurtful though well-intentioned modesty with which we say, "Oh no, I couldn't possibly," when someone has poured his heart into a desire to bless us. Of course, that's a lighter application than when referring to eternal grace and glory, but we can multiply it exponentially in accordance with the circumstances. God has poured His life, His entire creation intention, into loving us, and He carries His love for us as His yearning. Even in our imperfect human compassion for one another, we long to see each other's hopes and hearts fulfilled. How much greater should the desire be to see God's hope fulfilled, especially when that hope is for our sake in the first place?

There's a poem called "Almost Gone," which deals with the common struggle of fully accepting grace and captures the "embarrassment" of facing the undeserved perfection of grace. One particular portion of the poem states this concept bluntly, saying:

Lord, what nature of sin have you covered
under angels' wings?
In what clean cloak this
sinner wrongly bound?
But You are not wrong. Your mercy, which I know, is
beyond what I will ever understand.
If I were right, then in *my* mercy, I would take
myself from You.
But I am not right.
You are right, and You bind me in love,
and I thank this God that does these things.[1]

If the inclination to resist grace seems like an extremist, frail, emotional human concept, well, first of all, it is. But second, it's also biblical. The whole struggle, from start to finish, unfolds between Christ and Peter in John 13:6-9, when Peter, having watched Jesus wash the feet of his contemporaries, is now approached with the same and begins both to question and to resist:

He came to Simon Peter, who said to him, "Lord, are
you going to wash my feet?"
Jesus replied, "You do not realize now what I am doing,
but later you will understand."

"No," said Peter, "you shall never wash my feet."

Jesus answered, "Unless I wash you, you have no part
with me."

"Then, Lord," Simon Peter replied, "not just my feet
but my hands and my head as well!"

In that passage lies the completed picture of the human struggle with the grace of God. Peter had just watched Jesus washing,
by choice, the other disciples' feet, "cleansing the sin" of the
world around him. But, when it comes to individual salvation,
that's where the resistance comes in. "Not my feet," we say. Jesus even took the time to acknowledge our struggle, saying, "You
do not realize now what I am doing, but later you will understand" (13:7).

When we read the timeless progression in those verses, perhaps we can see ourselves. But we'll also see the whole struggle
represented, from not understanding God's grace, to resisting
when invited to receive it, to recognizing that rejecting it is calling God "wrong" and finally to accepting grace in the fullest,
most unwavering way. Grace is a manifestation of pure, unselfish, *agape* love, a combination of the human and the divine which
then becomes all divine.

It's why we're here, which brings us to the most important issue regarding the acceptance of grace. A new friend recently
asked me, just for the sake of conversation, "Why would we have
to be here (as in subjected to the terms of earth while God is in
His heaven) at all?" If it's a test of our response to God, why
would it be here, under such "unfair" and distorted circumstances, where it's so easy, if you're not seeking Him, to simply
not believe? Why here, where it's so easy to struggle with grace?

Good question. It was one I'd never had a sufficient answer
to, until that conversation, when the best guess I could muster
came out: We know from what He's said, done, proven—all undeserved, by the way (see Psalms 14:1-3; 53:1-3; Ecclesiastes

7:20; Romans 3:12)—that He loves us. *I created you, I lived and died for you, I endured the affliction of all your sin as My own so you wouldn't know the pain of a separation you can't imagine from where you stand. And, most of all, I am* here, *right now. All of this to prove that I love you. Now, you have one life in which to decide if you love Me.*

One life in which to decide if we love Him. But what it comes back to time and time again is that we, as a society in general, buck against being asked to have faith in Him under *worldly* conditions. Oh, but catch this, *He* has had faith in *us* under *heavenly* conditions, which is so much harder to do!

You have one life in which
to decide if you love Me.

Having faith in One so deserving of it should be an effortless task compared to God having faith in us, who have done nothing sufficient for Him and who so pale in the light of heaven and pure love. Yet He does. Under heavenly conditions, He has faith in us.

We may have questions about Him, but He has none about us. He doesn't struggle with accepting us. He is sure of His love; He is sure that it's us in His heart. He has decided. Now it's our turn. Under earthly conditions, will we have faith in Him? Will we accept His grace?

Reflections

1. What do you find to be the most difficult part of accepting God's grace? Is there something that hinders you from receiving His grace in full?

2. Are you measuring grace by *your* worth, or by His?
3. Are you sure of His grace? Under earthly conditions, will you have faith in Him?

Prayer

Lord, I will never fully understand what You have done for me, much less why. It's just not possible for the human mind to entirely comprehend Your grace. But when my lack of understanding begins to weaken my acceptance of Your grace, rescue me from myself. When I "shrink from grace" help me to see that I'm only shrinking from You. Help me to see how much Your heart aches with the distance between us, a distance You've already crossed but which I deny with my doubt, guilt and shame. With wide eyes, knowing yet unashamed, I want to hand You what You already know and have already conquered. Let me take joy in trading my sorrows for what You long to offer. Let me live the life You want me to, the one You bought and secured. Let me be free indeed and enjoy that liberty, holding Your hand, knowing the gift in whole has come from You. Let me live out grace. Amen.

Note

1. Amy Bartlett, "Almost Gone," New York, NY, 1997.

10

Get to the Cross

"If anyone would come after me, he must deny himself and take up his cross daily and follow me." (Luke 9:23)

My pastor is currently going through a series called "Turning Points in Jesus' Ministry." One recent Sunday, as I sat in my padded chair (the contemporary Californian version of a pew), I listened to the description of Jesus standing silently before Pontius Pilate, a vital and stirring point in His ministry, and one that required His silence when there was so much that could have been said. But Christ was faithful to what was required of Him in that moment, for the sake of what would come. He did what He had to, to get to the cross.

From there I walked the *Via Dolorosa* backward to where Jesus carried His cross, still silent to the crowds of mocking condemnation. It was enough that God, in His mercy, stepped down from His seat in glory simply to rescue us in love. It was enough that the Almighty, the I AM, the one who is the satisfaction of all need, cloaked Himself in the baseness of humanity and willingly became needful, hungry, vulnerable to pain. It was enough that He came at all. And then we spat at Him and cursed Him, the one who, at that moment, was providing salvation for us all.

My heart complained from my seat, *Why?* It was the same question I asked in earlier pages: "How could You, in all Your knowledge, not cry out the truth? How could You not silence the crowd with Your simple holiness?" I didn't expect an answer, but sometimes the Lord seems to answer the rhetorical questions more quickly than the ones to which we expect an answer. He explained, *I had to get to the cross.*

At first I thought I was having the same conversation I'd had a million times, always accepting though never understanding how He could have loved us enough to stay silent while perfection was wrongly accused and convicted. But this time it seemed that He was saying more. He was saying everything, and His answer began to play in wide-screen excellence through my mind.

We lock ourselves behind a million gates with nothing more powerful than thought to hold us there.

Every moment, every turning point of ministry, every breath and word that was His, was in order for Him to get to the cross, and it is my task in life to do the same. My every word, hope, breath, decision large and small, my *every* turning point of ministry, is to get to the cross. Get to where the gospel happens. Get to where Jesus is going. Get into God's plan and trust it, no matter where it looks like it's going from where you stand. In Jesus' perfectly patterned example, trust your Father.

There was a moment for Christ when getting to where He knew He needed to be meant walking straight into the darkness, even feeling "forsaken" by the One He glorified as He died. There were times for Him when getting there meant weeping, times when it meant preaching loudly from the hillside, times when it meant silence—not a single word. There were times when it meant a righteous anger, times of prayer and pleading, times of promise and celebration, times of preparing and times of walking. But notice both fulfillments: First, that the purpose of everything He did was to get to the cross, and second, that He did anything necessary to get to the cross.

That's our task and privilege now, through the strength and guiding of His Spirit. The purpose of everything we do should be to get to the cross, and we must do whatever it takes in the moment to get there, whether it be through silence, preaching, love or prayer. For some it has even meant death. While for most of us it's unlikely that we'll ever be called to choose between life and our faith, we're still commanded in the Scripture to love not our lives "so much as to shrink from death" (Revelation 12:11). However this translates to your circumstances, determine to get there.

And while we're gauging the steps to the cross, ours and His, we must count the ones already taken. The road to Golgotha was called the *Via Dolorosa*, the way of pain, and most often this is the nature of path-to-Calvary references—that we must be willing to face the toughest journey for the sake of the cross. But be careful not to miss the victory and joy of that road, which is also both His and ours.

Because of that road, we have freedom, but we may have difficulty accepting it. As Jean-Paul Sartre wrote, "Hell's gates are locked willingly from the inside." It's easy to skip over that sentence if we're thinking of it only in application to salvation, but it's not just an insight offered to those yet to take hold of Christ's saving grace. It's about whatever withholds us from the whole of Him, in whatever manner, today. It's what keeps us from fully realizing and appreciating the fact that He has paid the price to unlock the gate.

We lock ourselves behind a million gates with nothing more powerful than thought to keep us there. There are smaller, more temporary hells that we lock ourselves into daily—perpetual sadness, deafness to the Shepherd's calls, other loves and things that feign comfort. Even with an open door, the empty air around us becomes dead-bolted by doubt and padlocked by fear and failure. We fail to acknowledge the steps He has already taken in getting us to the cross.

Emotions can be one of the biggest barriers between us and knowing the fullness of God in the moment. Our emotions are not only deceptive; they are also deceived themselves, a result of the lies of Satan that tear us down or turn us away from the things of God. "The heart is deceitful above all things" (Jeremiah 17:9). We must remember that every single element that matters regarding God is, in its purest form, not an emotion. Faith, trust, obedience, willingness, etc. are choices. They are decisions, constant opportunities to place our faith to the left or to the right. When we just state what we know is truth, regardless of our mismatched emotions, we can watch the fact of that truth follow.

It's so much easier to wait for the lie to pass when you know that the Truth is coming.

When you can't find your trust, just *tell* Him, "I *will* trust You. I don't feel trust, but I choose it. I can't see how You're going to work this one out, especially 'for good' (see Romans 8:28), but I know You, so I defy my feelings and I determine that I will trust You."

When you don't *feel* the comfort of God's words, at least remember the *fact* of them. Lean into the knowledge of the promise of them. Remember that emotions are most often simply moods, easily defeatable by time, much more by God's healing might. "Weeping may endure for a night, but joy cometh in the morning" (Psalm 30:5, KJV).

The first or second or twentieth time you've been through an attack of this sort—being deceived by emotions, circumstances, Satan, and losing sight of God's promises—you might wonder if you're going to make it through to morning without your heart breaking in two. But then you learn that the lies of Satan can disappear as quickly as they've come in, and it's so much easier to wait for the lie to pass when you know that the Truth is coming. Don't let your heart break. It's such a waste when true joy is within heart's reach and has been paid for. It was such a large price, won with every moment of the life of Jesus, won in the heart of God when He knew He would give His own Son. Won in silence, preaching, weeping, praying, laughing, healing, living and dying.

Christ won it with His death. Give it your life. Keep walking the road. Get to the cross. Whatever it takes, get to the cross. He will see you safely home.

Reflections

1. What are some of the emotions with which you struggle the most?
2. What gets your blood boiling too hastily, "pushes your buttons"? What can you do in the moment to remember to grope for God's reaction instead of yours?
3. What stones are in your path as you try to get to the cross today?

Prayer

Lord, whatever it is that stands between me and Your cross today, remove it. Whatever keeps me from You, whatever keeps me from living Your light, wipe it out. Protect me from what would come to distract, destroy, blind or worry my heart—even that which comes from within me, a result of my poor choices. Wipe clean my eyes, sharpen my hearing, strengthen my hand. Awaken me, walk with me, get me to Calvary, Lord. Pull me to You and let me stand by You, that I may be a strength to others on the way. You carried a cross that was mine, Lord. It's such a small task, now, for me to carry this lesser one on earth. Let me do everything I can, and let nothing stand between me and living entirely with You, for You, because of You, today. Amen.

11

Uf You Love Me

I have made you known to them, and will continue to make you known in order that the love you have for me may be in them and that I myself may be in them. (John 17:26)

t was business that brought me to their home the first time and love that brought me back. After a couple years of being a frail little boat in a very forceful urban sea, unable even to find a solid church family, I found a gentle sanctuary of spiritual support in one family's home in Watertown, New York. They lived six hours to the north of me, but it was a far cry closer than the 3,000 miles that separated me from my "real" family.

I was in college at the time, and so little of what I had within my grasp was worth holding on to. I had been tossed into a city where a lot of what you encounter you don't want to hold on to, but the worthlessness of what I held was mostly because I wasn't reaching for God.

Two years into my time in college, God began to turn the tides. I went to Watertown, just shy of the Canadian border, and met that family, who would be my hosts while I was in town for an event. I knew God had arranged a meeting of purpose when their little girl answered the door in a yellow T-shirt that said, "Jesus Loves You." I knew He loved me, but I had struggled so hard that I was barely holding on to the truth of those words.

It only took a week (though a day would have had the same effect) for Dave and Gail and Christine Goings, the little girl at the door, to become family to me. They were going to be permanent. They were going to be a portion of my restoration.

The first evening I was in their home we sang "Amazing Grace" sitting on the living room rug, and I remembered that "the city" was not the rest of the world. I rested in the comfort of that household, and by the time I had to go back to the city, I'd set my sights on different goals. I realized I had forgotten temporarily to take the promises of the Bible literally—the lion's den (see Daniel 6), the figure of the fourth in the fire (see Daniel 3). I had given up without trying, and I hadn't even noticed that I'd done so.

*My life would not only be about Christ,
but about anyone who crossed my path
long enough to scribble his name into my heart.*

As I was leaving, the Goings gave me a little red New Testament that was about the size of my hand. It seemed like the heavens opened up and shone on my new little Bible. It wasn't the Bible itself; I had one of my own at home, one I loved even more, which had been a gift from my parents (who knew what I'd soon face) when I left for school and New York. With the red New Testament, it was the *moment* that the gift represented that mattered. It was the recognition of a life I could have, a life I had no idea I was slowly losing. God's message to me was as clear as a phone call: *Amy, it's Me. It may be a long journey, but I'm going to begin to send you everything you need to get home to Me.* Little did I know that I would eventually go far beyond "home" into a life greater than anything I'd thus far imagined.

That New Testament was my life raft, and as I climbed onto the Amtrak Special that would take me back to the city, I held on to the gift as such. My treasure. My beginning.

I went off to the dining car for a cup of coffee, encouraged, inspired, thirsty. I was joined almost immediately by a briefcase thrown on my table followed by a businessman who had been traveling for far too long and drinking far too much. The scent of bourbon preceded his introduction and lingered as he got comfortable, got personal and then got aberrant at the sight of my New Testament sitting behind my coffee cup. After a one-sided religious debate and a few last-ditch come-ons, he got up to leave, and I let down my guard long enough to miss the fact that he'd grabbed my new Bible and was writing his name and number in black ballpoint ink across the inside front cover.

I was immaturely devastated. I later tried desperately to erase the writing, to scrub the blemish away. The book was a material object, so the whole situation was ultimately a small bother, but I considered my gift ruined to a degree. Smeared.

I didn't dwell on it, but several years later the illustration finally reached me: That man, the stereotype of the drunken businessman on a train, had not tainted my Bible—neither the literal gift nor the symbolism of it. Rather, he blessed it, perfected it, clarified the larger message behind its symbolism. I realized that, ideally, my life would not only be about Christ, but about anyone who crossed my path long enough to scribble his name into my heart. I wouldn't erase a single one. I would remember the urgency with which God loves each one and purpose to tell all of them with my life that God is singularly devoted to them. My life would go so much further than simply coming back to rest in God; it would enthusiastically, unrestrainedly spill over into the bigger purpose behind His love: others.

The blemish I'd lamented—a drunken man's phone number, the pink smear of eraser rubber, neither one removable—was now the gem that completed the full message behind that Watertown Bible. It was a promise of what my life would be around the bend, of the nearness of the Lord, the assuredness of the gospel, the renewal and relief of it all and the resulting urgency to pass it on.

There's a country song that's been playing on the radio lately that admittedly makes me cry like a girl. It's called "Three Wooden Crosses,"[1] and like all good country songs it has a surprise in the last verse. The song is about four people on a bus—a preacher, a teacher, a farmer and a prostitute. There's an accident, and three of those lives are lost. Then the verse goes on to tell what each person left behind. The farmer's legacy had been raising his son to love God and to nurture the land God gave them. The teacher left behind the impact she'd made on the children she had taught. And then the scene plays out between the preacher and the prostitute in which the preacher lays a "bloodstained Bible" in the prostitute's hands and whispers, "Can't you just see the Promised Land?" We assume that phrase is the pastor's message of love and assurance of Jesus to the dying prostitute because the song later reveals that this story is being told by a preacher behind the pulpit who is holding the same bloodstained Bible.

The twist comes when the preacher goes on to explain that the Bible was given to him by his mother, who had received it from the dying preacher years ago. It was the preacher who had died, not the prostitute, and in taking his last moment of life to "promise Jesus" to someone, that person's life was changed, as well as the life of her child and all those whom that child would then reach with God's love.

What makes me cry, for reasons much larger than the song, is the weakened heart exulting, "Can't you just see the Promised Land?" It sings of the last moment of life, unshaken by the darkness of unavoidable death, alive with the promise of life in Jesus. Not only unshaken but inspired by that love to the last, enough to say with joy and passion, "Look! See Him!"

In my book *Be Still America . . . I Am God* there is a story of a man whose ability to share the gospel I aim to emulate. On one of his frequent business flights, Rev. William Faye reached out to a particular flight attendant and led her to Christ before they landed. He exchanged information with her and kept in contact—but only for a few weeks. She was a member of the crew on one of the four planes that went down on September 11, 2001.

Urgency is always present in this life. The Lord is calling, longing to know and to love those who would willingly love Him, willing that "all men would be saved" (see 1 Timothy 2:4). Jesus, in one of His own last earthly moments, sat and shared the epitome of His heart with Peter, asking him three times, "Peter, do you love me?"

If you love Him, feed His lambs.

"Yes Lord, you *know* that I do." Peter answered the question each time with increasing earnestness.

Jesus met that earnestness with His own. Changing His words with every response, getting the message all the way through, Jesus charged, "Feed my lambs." "Take care of my sheep." "Feed my sheep" (John 21:15-19). "If you love me," He was saying to Peter, "you'll do what My heart cries for. You'll tell them, Peter, that I love them."

If you love Him, feed His lambs, take care of His sheep, feed His sheep. Do all that is best for them, and make their care your priority, your earnest response to Jesus' heart-cry. If you love Him, tell them.

And "Rick," from the Amtrak Special, thank you for the lesson you could never know you taught me. I'm sorry I didn't tell you how much He loves you too.

Reflections

1. Are you sensitive to moments when others are in need of Christ? Are you willing to respond to them?
2. Actively ask God to bring to you those He knows are in need of His love, those He's trying to reach. Ask the Lord to fill you with *His* hunger to reach them.
3. Was there a chance to tell someone about Christ, or simply to reach out in His love, that you know you missed? Is it possible to go back to that person? If not, what can you do to recognize and respond to the moment next time?
4. Have you gotten far away from something that God wants for your life? Is there a call you've been hearing to come nearer to the Lord to which you haven't yet responded?

Prayer

Lord, I have heard You calling so many times, and I have ignored You. But persist, Lord, when I am deaf. Keep after me. And light that fire within me to help others to hear You calling. I don't think any of us grasps the weight of eternity. We know that we must seek You while You can still be found, that it can be too late at any moment. Why then, Lord, is it so easy for us to be so quiet, so slow to tell others about You? Let me use my every breath to be the sound of Your familiar voice to all those You would love. Let no one within my reach ever want for the light of Your love. Let everything I am and everything I do speak constantly to my own heart and to everyone I encounter, "Can't you just see the Promised Land?" Amen.

Note

1. Randy Travis, *Rise and Shine*, Warner Bros. Records, Inc., 2002.

12

Preach It

*And I will ask the Father, and he will give you another Counselor
to be with you forever—the Spirit of truth. The world cannot accept him, because it neither sees him nor knows him. But you know
him, for he lives with you and will be in you. (John 14:16-17)*

*He said to them, "Go into all the world and preach the good news
to all creation." (Mark 16:15)*

I was working a temp job at the FDIC in New York City. Jobs
like these can be especially tough for the artistic soul, but in
the attitude of "all things as unto the Lord" (see 1 Corinthians
10:31), I took on the tasks of crunching numbers, answering
phones and, more than the rest of my responsibilities, making
friends with the security guards across from my desk. There
could be no joy for me in a ledger, so I knew there had to be a
greater reason that I was there (as is true no matter where we
are: God wastes no plan). So I prayed, "Lord, let Your light shine
from this desk. Use me here."

I had been on the job three days when a conversation about
the Holy Spirit broke out around the security desk. The security
guards asked me what "side" I took on the subject. I spoke without apology and left what I said in the Lord's hands. By lunch-
time, five or six random employees had gathered, and the

conversation had intensified into a passionate discussion not
only about the Holy Spirit, but about the Trinity, God's love and
power as they are available in the present day and the concept of
absolute truth. Both "sides" of the discussion were well represented, but the Lord's side was gently prevailing. The debaters
kept shouting across the corridor to get me to weigh in. This, at
the front entrance to the New York offices of the FDIC.

I had only asked for a mild opportunity to represent my faith.
A nice, easy "Hey, do you believe in God?" at the water cooler.
This was years ago when I was just getting my "Jesus feet" beneath me. I'd learned nothing yet about the gentle authority of
the Holy Spirit that takes over when there's someone He's trying
to reach. That's what He was doing there on the nineteenth floor
of the FDIC building: moving in lives, taking His rightful place as
Truth.

Scared by what was still such a new experience for me, I pan-
icked in the elevator as I took my lunch break. I was like a kid in a
kindergarten play whispering to Dad in the audience, "How'm I
doin'?" only I was more troubled, sure that I'd botched the job.
"Did I go overboard, Lord? I don't know how this goes yet. Was
it me or was it You? Was it too much for a place of business? Was
I too adamant about an absolute truth and not sensitive enough
to their views?"

Faithful and eager to answer someone who seeks Him in this
manner, someone who wants to learn how to speak His name and is
searching for the balance of the Great Commission, God took no
more than five minutes to stamp a solid answer on my questions.
Once I'd reached the street, I got a hot dog and started across the
road to the library to sit on the steps in the sun. Halfway across Fifth
Avenue, I stopped dead in my tracks, sauerkraut falling in the cross-
walk, autumn air stinging my eyes, which had fixed on the north end
of the library wall where my answer was written in stone: "Above all
things, truth beareth away the victory."

I was only beginning to learn that the boundaries I thought were situated—culturally, professionally and personally—didn't exist when it comes to God's Spirit at work. There is a balance and a decency, sure. Mild is fine when it's time. Even Jesus was silent when it mattered for Him to be so. But sometimes we shut His mouth *for* Him; sometimes we shut Him out. So while there's a balance between modesty and audacity, we most often tilt that balance too far away from Him.

Above all things, truth beareth away the victory.

For decades, we've upset this balance in the media. There are secular arenas where we're not allowed to say "Jesus." Why? We can say anything else we like. There are curse words in kids' films like *Antz* and *The Grinch*. Yet there are certain places where we're told that faith doesn't belong. Really? That's news to God, who's there already, waiting.

What's most frustrating of all is that one of the "groups" that is most to blame for this tilt away from God is the body of believers, soft-spoken Christians who often apologize for having to apologize for our faith, while everyone else fights for their rights—constitutional, human, civil.

We need to realize that the rug of Judeo-Christian values *could* be pulled completely out from under the foundation of this nation if we don't begin to speak up and to "live" Jesus. There's no great mystery to figuring out how to tilt the balance back in the right direction. Finding a balance of unapologetic truth and unadulterated, agape love was both modeled by and achieved in Christ.

Run while time can be had, and tell people who loves them, who has paid the price for their names, who waits for them. There is no time to ask, "But what is it, Lord, that You want us to do?" He's already answered that question: *Preach it.* That answer is not "religion" or good deeds. It's not just about a sociopolitical climate or American (or global) history. It's a handclasping, eye-locking decree. It's one of the last things He said before He left this earth and left us to task with His talents in our hands (see Matthew 25:14-30). Do not bury them. You think He was upset to see metaphoric gold coins buried and wasted? Imagine His response to the waste of burying His Son.

And that's the thing: You can't bury Jesus. You can stick Him in the tomb all you want, but He will rise and deliver salvation with or without you. You can be there running ahead, saying, "I've seen Him. I've touched His wounds. He lives!" Or you can be the one who stuck Him in the tomb, scratching your head, wondering how He got out. But you can't bury the gospel.

Come and see what the Lord has done!

We worry about getting "preachy" nowadays, but since when did that become a bad word or take on a negative connotation? Just because there are poor examples of "preachy" in the media, or because some have come with insincere motives and been exposed, doesn't mean that we should be enticed to drop the mantle. We say, "I don't want to get preachy here," after Jesus says, "Go and *preach* the gospel" (see Matthew 28:19-20; Mark 13:10).

Preach it. Speak up. We've already talked about the importance and urgency of Christ's plea to "tell them." After exploring the "inspiration" to tell the world and answering the question, "Do you *want* to tell them?" the question here goes one step further into, "*Will* you tell them?" And not just of salvation, but of all His works, strengths and promises for every day.

My family had a rainbow at our house the other day. We often do. My mother says we have a "good rainbow location." But this particular rainbow was extraordinary, and it had us running, calling to one another from different points in the house, racing from the backyard to the front and back again. It was a full semi-circle rainbow, one end to the other, and a double! I laughed at us, because I couldn't remember the last time something made us all run like that, together.

But in the middle of that thought, I saw the whole picture, the symbolism of all the doors in the house being wide open, us calling one another's names with uncommon gleeful expressions like, "Oh my goodness, look, look! Have you ever seen such a thing? It's incredible," then taking it up an octave and a decibel and repeating the whole phrase again. When was the last time we pointed out God's handiwork to one another at all, much less with so much astonishment and joy? It's a conventional illustration, nonetheless precise: A rainbow is God's promise stretched across the sky. But we also need to realize that daily He stretches promises across our lives. If we could put on our rainbow-colored spectacles and see God's handiwork for the miracle it is, we would just as enthusiastically shout to those around us, "Come and see what the Lord has done!"

Don't be afraid to point out the beauty of the Lord, for He is beautiful and His promises are true, without contest. But most of all, His Spirit is working—with or without us, though according to Him, He'd prefer it be *through* us. So all that's left is for us to join Him where He's already working. It's actually less of a bold pioneer endeavor than we paint it to be, less daunting and so much more powerful—there is more at stake, more possible—than we could ever imagine. You don't have to be the picture of a warrior; just don't close the door. Meet Him there and let Him be Jesus.

Reflections

1. Do you believe that God's Word is absolutely true? If you do, are you willing to stand behind it when someone challenges it or quietly questions the truth of God?
2. Can you recall a situation in which you noticed yourself biting your tongue when you had a chance to speak up in favor of God? In what environments are you most apprehensive about mentioning God?
3. Is there someone on your heart with whom you feel God is leading you to share His love? What are some ways you can practice following the nudges of the Holy Spirit to speak His name?

Prayer

Lord, it can be hard in this world to understand the balance of loving one another and loving You, as we sometimes think there's a difference between the two. But You have already given us a perfect model of how we are to speak, live and love, and all of this in You, in Your perfect character. Make me unwaveringly like You. Give me a reality of love and a reality of truth, and let me hold fast to both. Make me bold in the faith with which You've entrusted me, but let me be so without a hint of any of it coming from me. When I am brave enough to speak Your name, take over. Stand behind Your truth at every moment. In this world, Father, Your truth is contested constantly and skewed; even evil is spoken in Your name, at times even by me and my best intentions. I know I am not always the brightest example of You, but shine more brightly, Lord, even in my faults. Shine blindingly against what tries to crucify Your name. Take any trembling effort of faith, especially against adversity, and make it a wave of Your very own hand, a sweet fragrance, an incontestable word. Amen.

13

In the Company of Help

The LORD upholds all those who fall
and lifts up all who are bowed down.
The eyes of all look to you,
and you give them their food at the proper time.
You open your hand
and satisfy the desires of every living thing.
The LORD is righteous in all his ways
and loving toward all he has made.
The LORD is near to all who call on him,
to all who call on him in truth.
He fulfills the desires of those who fear him;
he hears their cry and saves them. (Psalm 145:14-19)

I've been up in the hills of northern California laying down the foundations for this book. After spending ten years in New York City, I'm overcompensating by spending most of my time outside, breathing deeply. I spend the days poring over the view like a good book: a hawk on stock-still wings, searching; foothills folded like passive hands, with just a budding camisole of spring; and in the pasture beside me, a few cows and goats I've grown to know, and one lone donkey.

It was the donkey that caught my attention when I first arrived. It was his surprising, abstract beauty that I noticed; he was scruffy, out of place, lacking sculpture, but somehow perfect in his imperfection. He pales in comparison to the roan thoroughbreds at the bottom of the hill, perfect accessories to a sunlit farm. Their backs glint copper even from this distance. The donkey stands beside me with matted, muddied hair and odd ears that twitch with embarrassment when he hears his own voice. I was sure a devotional was hidden in him, the chosen steed of the Lord. But the story God began to present to me was not the obvious one. (I should have known.) Instead, the story was a four-day goat saga, a setup from the Lord from the very beginning.

What brought tears to my eyes were their eyes trained on me directly.

Day one, 8:00 a.m., loose goat. Now, it's not my goat, not my house, not my pasture, and it's way too early in the morning for fast thinking. But in my sleepy estate, I heard a goat bleating urgently (believe me, there's a difference between a normal bleat and an urgent bleat) at the bottom of the driveway. I found shoes (not even mine), stumbled outside and found a gate. I discovered that the gate wasn't locked, only closed with a tricky knot in the chain, so I opened the gate and maneuvered the loose goat back into the pasture. I was a proud farmer; there was no city girl here.

The goat called to its friends in a new tone of bleat that had changed from the former, a downright detectable call for help, to more of a "you guys wouldn't believe what just happened to me" bleat. That's when I noticed that this goat was a mama. A gorgeous black baby goat, who was still nursing, ran to feed from her reunited parent.

That would've been enough adventure with the farm animals for me, but the next morning, the exact same thing happened, and then again later that evening. By the third time, the goat had figured out where her help was coming from and had the boldness to walk all the way up to the edge of my stairs calling, "Help!" (I was learning to speak the language.) I let her back into the pasture one last time and called her owners to figure out why she kept getting out.

Before I knew it, I was getting a twenty-year history of each animal in the field from a man who truly cared for his animals. I could hear that he honestly understood and had adopted God's command to be responsible for all His creatures. The man wasn't just a farmer; he was cousin to Adam, lovingly doing his job. He told me about the goats' recent bout with pneumonia, why they sounded different and that I needn't worry about any of them . . . except maybe the old brown one. She was two decades old and was expected to topple over pretty soon.

That's why I was all the more concerned the next morning when, through the window, I saw a very frail brown goat caught upside down on the hill, neck in the fence, only hurting herself further as she struggled to get loose. I ran to the edge of the field, reached through the fence and uprighted her. But she still couldn't stand and began to slip down the hill again. With no time to get to the gate, I climbed the old, rattling fence, laughing at the thought of the out-of-towner ending up speared on a fence post, the mistake of an amateur goatherd. I also wondered briefly, though without pause, how the cows and donkey would respond to my presence in the field. But the frightened goat beneath my hands made my own fears wane.

I leapt from the fence and sat with her for as long as it took for her to regain some strength. I felt her heartbeat as I lay my hand on her side and wished that God would take the poor thing home. Her stomach gurgled with something like age and fear as I read the faded etching on her collar. I decided I was too emotional to be a farmer. Finally the goat found tottering strength in her legs as I tried to lift her one last time, and she made it up the hill and away.

There were already a million angles for me to walk away with from my goat adventures on the farm, but the real fist to the heart was still on its way. Only a few minutes later I poured a hot cup of coffee and found a seat outside in the sun, waking slowly, letting the "emergency status" which had brought me into the day dissipate. Their breakfast over, the animals began to disappear one by one over the edge of the hill. I lingered, I read, I sipped. I watched the trains going in and out of the hills, my familiar Union Pacific and its mountain-bound whistle call. So grateful and calmly contented, my gaze drifted down from the high tracks back into the pasture, where all the animals had finally left—except for two.

About ten yards away, two goats were sitting in the sun with me, legs folded beneath them, their gaze turned precisely in my direction. For a moment, I thought nothing more than, *Why didn't they follow their fellows away over the hill like they do every other morning?*—until I noticed which goats they were. It was the old brown goat on my right and the mama, with the unmistakably identifying black spot across her back, to my left. More poignantly, it was the lost one and the fallen one. We made a perfect triangle, the three of us, with a short but tender history. And I almost hadn't noticed, but there on the other side of the mama was her kid. The parent's focus was becoming the child's. (Raise them "in the way [they] should go" [Proverbs 22:6].)

But what brought tears to my eyes were *their* eyes—notably unavoidable, wide, brown goat eyes—trained on me directly. It wasn't the attention or the personal glory that moved me; it was the clear voice of God that began to speak to my heart, recognizably, ready for me to learn. It was the caring plea from Him, calling for me to understand Him, to know Him and to lean into His helping hand. Just as when you begin to piece together what someone must have gone through to plan a gift or a surprise for you, I was touched to discover what He'd known all week, what He'd been planning with every progression of the story.

Look at their eyes, He said to my heart. *They don't move; they don't even wander. They know you care, know you will help. When the others have gone, they remain with you because they know how it feels to be saved.*

The ones who remained were those who had seen trouble and had been saved.

I wasn't sure if it was gratitude in their eyes or if they just liked the sense of security, or perhaps even the company. But they clearly understood that I cared, and, very simply, they were there. When all the rest had gone away, the ones who remained were those who had seen trouble and had been saved, the ones who had gotten themselves in a fix, through foolhardiness or weakness or, if I equate myself, sheer stupidity at times. They were the ones who knew what it was to be helped and loved, and they wisely sat down in the company of help.

I don't know if goats are capable of love or gratitude, but I am. So how much more should I remain, with my eyes fixed upon my Help? *I hear You, Lord,* my heart whispered on its own as I trained my heart-sight on Him and lifted my eyes, quite literally, to the hills. *I* know *where my help comes from* (see Psalm 121:1).

Reflections

1. What are you most grateful to the Lord for today? In your life as a whole?
2. Have you sat with Him lately and given Him your company in affectionate appreciation?
3. When you encounter a need, how long does it take you to call to God for help?

Prayer

Lord, I will stay constantly in Your company. I will watch You. I have learned, especially through my foolhardiness and weaknesses, that You care, that You are my help and my salvation, that You have even knelt to call me "friend." I have learned that You are at my side, waiting, when I have fallen and am far too weak to stand. My Lord, who sits both on the throne and in the dirt with me, lift me again to my feet, and I will stay fixed on You, watching You, learning. You are my winning hope. I am learning how greatly You are my savior. Amen.

14

Chosen Company

Seek the LORD while he may be found;
call on him while he is near. (Isaiah 55:6)

was stranded in Chicago, alone and slightly bored. Bored in Chicago? As unbelievable as that might sound, it's possible when you have no company. But "no company," I later learned, was part of a perfect design. I'd been leaning on other people too hard for too long, and was unaware that the arm that leaned on Jesus was becoming a little weak. God was preparing both remedy and rescue, and it began with my being alone.

Earlier in the day I'd gone to Pacific Garden Mission (PGM) on State Street, a place I love to visit whenever I'm in the Windy City. I wanted to catch their service, which I remembered being at 6:30 p.m. Services aren't necessarily open to the public, but I know a few people who work there, and I was hoping just to be allowed to stand in the back. It is always a privilege and a fresh reminder of my own weaknesses to be anywhere near a PGM service with those men who have absolutely nothing left, nothing but Jesus, and yet stand on their feet just to thank God for the day and for the chance to sing His praises.

I took a cab to get there on time, but when I got there the room was empty. I learned that services had been moved to 8:00 p.m. I left, a little disappointed. It was dark, and now I had *nothing* to do.

For nearly two hours I walked around Chicago. It was hard to enjoy the restaurants as a party of one. There were all sorts of places I simply didn't want to go to alone, and the well lit places were closed. Even the Starbucks closed at five.

When I'd finally given up on exploring the metropolis, I thought that at the very least I could pick up a few things at the local drug store, maybe have a long conversation with a friend on my "unlimited weekend minutes" and call room service. But as I browsed there in the Walgreens, arms full of junk food, neck bent with cell phone between ear and shoulder, even those plans fell through. The friend I'd called asked if he could call me back in an hour, just as the manager of the store came to tell me they were closing in five minutes. At 8 o'clock in the evening? Even the drug store had abandoned me. No shopping. No phone call. I could not in clear conscience go back to my hotel room at 8 p.m. knowing that was the last of Chicago I'd see in ages. Surely there had to be *something* to appreciate at that hour. "Lord," I prayed jokingly, "Send me someone to play with!"

Clear as a bell, in my heart I heard Him say, *Come play with Me!* There was excitement in the whisper, and I laughed, thinking the lesson was that He was my joy and my company at all times in all circumstances. And that *was* the lesson, ultimately, but He meant it literally too. So again His response came, *No, really. Come play with Me!*

That's when the exclamation point landed. The services I'd sought earlier and disappointingly missed, the ones that had been moved to eight, were starting now, only blocks away. I hailed a cab and told the driver I was in a hurry, giggling like I was nuts, wishing I had the guts to say, "And step on it! I'm meeting God there." I laughed out loud at the thought, and the driver checked me in the rearview mirror.

When I arrived at the mission, everyone I knew had left for the day, and no one would let me into the service for security reasons. Just imagine the visual, me standing unchaperoned in the back of a room filled with about 300 of Chicago's most homeless. Those men are gems for the most part, but the mission couldn't be held liable for the exceptions. That's when Miracle Number Two came in and asked me if I wanted to join a few visiting members of a nearby church who were seated on the stage. I didn't want to make a scene, but there was a side entrance to the stage and an open chair a few feet from that door. "I'd love that, thank you."

Clear as a bell, in my heart I heard Him say, "Come play with Me!"

I must have looked stupidly happy in my tattered chair, trying to quietly tuck beneath it the few bags of goodies I'd managed to gather before the Walgreens closed. Plastic bags don't tuck quietly, but the music started and took the attention away from my disruption. Someone handed me a hymnal and I wanted to cry.

Now, lest you think I'm exaggerating or way too thrilled by a chance to be in church, as if I lived in a land where it were forbidden, let me clarify: It was the message of individual, desired love that floored me in that moment. *Me,* He'd harkened. *Come take joy in Me.*

As much as I wanted company in general—or as much as I wanted certain people's company—God desires mine to an unfathomable degree more. He misses me, He loves me, He pursues me—all of us—in this manner, and we take it for granted, always replacing Him with lesser loves, poorer fulfillments, other company. He wants us to want His company as much as He wants ours, and certainly more than we want others' companionship.

I wanted to cry tears of joy. It was a reunion. I hadn't realized how far I'd inched away from seeking Him alone and being satisfied in it, how much I'd come to depend on the company and love of others and, as I said, how weak my arms were becoming because of it. I realized that there were things in my life that I hadn't even considered temptations or distractions—but aren't those "harmless" things the most powerful?

Do yourself a favor: For the sake of God, your heart and circumstances that can tumble out of hand like a wildfire after a long, dry year, leap to attention at the first sign of temptation or distraction. See it not for what it looks like at the moment, not as harmless or excusable; see it rather for what it can quickly become. Whether it's something serious that can pull you away from Him or something seemingly not so serious (but realistically just as dangerous) that misdirects your attention, take a deep breath and run. Run from what lures you, and run *to* Him who lovingly calls you.

> *When He calls, jump in a cab and meet Him there. Run to Him.*

He loves you so much. He longs for you so much. He calls to be with you. Yes, because He wants to heal, lead, save and work through your hands to reach the world. But don't forget it's also simply because He wants to *be* with you.

When He calls, jump in a cab and meet Him there. Run to Him. Just like I had been doing, we often and repeatedly lean on other people and things so heavily that we begin to forget His abundance, His love, the delight and perfection of His company alone. But regardless of our misplaced attentions, we are consistently Jesus' chosen company, and His arms never weaken as He pulls us ever back into His presence, safely "leaning, leaning, leaning on the Everlasting Arms."

It was the greatest night I'd ever spent in Chicago.

Reflections

1. Have you ever had a chance to make God's companionship your greatest joy? The next time you feel lonely, ask Him to be even more present. Ask Him how to be more than satisfied in His company alone.
2. How much do you long for Him compared to that which competes for the attention you should be giving Him?

Prayer

Lord, especially when we grow to depend too much on the tangible, it's hard for us to imagine being utterly contented in Your company. We so often make the mistake of thinking we're still alone and merely "helped through the aloneness" by the presence of a loving Holy Spirit. I know that You are with me when my heart is lonesome and that You will love me through that, but help me to appreciate Your lonesomeness for me and to respond. Help me to be satisfied entirely with Your companionship above all else. Show me what it can be like, Lord, to choose Your company and watch the world fade into second place. Never stop calling me to live in joy with You. Let me always respond to Your invitation to run to You, to be joyously at Your side, but let it always be on my lips to call You to me as well. Be my chosen company, Lord, and thank You that You make me Yours. Amen.

15

The Gift of Weakness

But he said to me, "My grace is sufficient for you, for my power is made perfect in weakness." Therefore I will boast all the more gladly about my weaknesses, so that Christ's power may rest on me. That is why, for Christ's sake, I delight in weaknesses, in insults, in hardships, in persecutions, in difficulties. For when I am weak, then I am strong. (2 Corinthians 12:9-10)

At writers' conferences I often ask members of the audience to raise their hands if they're weary, feeling unfit for the task, discouraged or ready to tell God "no," even uncharacteristically. In an environment like that, where the attendees have all been exploring their sensitive passions and having their explorations met with constructive criticism for days, every hand is raised. In response to the physicality of that admission, where they can "feel" their knowledge of their own weaknesses raised in disclosure over their heads, I tell them, "Good. Then you're exactly who God is looking for."

I challenge you to find a person in the Bible who, by his own rights and strengths, should have been chosen for the task he was given. Even beyond "should," there are few who didn't fight

God's call, didn't shake in their boots (or sandals) or explain to God gently but firmly how His plan was a mistake.

Moses balked and initially recoiled from his call. Yet despite his stuttering speech, he was made the voice that spoke the delivery of Israel. David was so under the standard for being a king that he wasn't even considered in the lot of candidates. Yet he was called in from the field, dirty and smelling like sheep, to be anointed on the spot for his coming calling as king, just fourteen generations shy of the day the Word became flesh.

Gideon was afraid despite constant reassurance from an Almighty God, and God never faulted him for it. In fact, even after wringing out fleeces and testing God again, Gideon received further instruction telling him what he could do if he was still afraid (see Judges 7:10-11). In the very next verse, he did what God suggested, indicating that, yes, he was still afraid. Yet God called Gideon "mighty warrior" before he had even done anything that might have earned him the title.

All these heroes were painfully aware of their inadequacies. They were frightened, unsure, incapable, underaccomplished . . . mighty warriors. It is the same with us today. Not only are we underqualified and afraid, but we argue with God. We try to refuse His calling, like Moses when he said, "Not me, Lord; I *can't.* I would if I could, but I *can't.*"

Well of *course* we can't, but that's not the question. As a matter of fact, throughout the Bible we see that God routinely chose those who cannot. If we could, God might have moved on to someone a little more *un*able.

I've learned to wear my "can't" like a badge. I've learned to smirk at the undoable, challenge the unlikely, roll my eyes at the improbable, saying, "Yes, Lord, I see You." Then I put on my life jacket and wait for the dam to break. My weakness has often launched my greatest adventures.

It is a proven part of God's formula that we would be weak, doubtful and afraid, that we would feel ill-equipped, overwhelmed and lost. If any of this is present in your life, it's the first sign that He's got plans for you. It's your claim to His strength. It wasn't without reason that He pledged that when we are weak, He would be strong (see 2 Corinthians 12:9).

The most complete description of the ultimate moment of weakness actually *being* the ultimate triumph of strength is Calvary itself, the incomparable darkness into which was birthed the conquering Light. It was the brokenness of Christ that won the wholeness of man, the adopted weakness of God being the strength that authored eternal victory.

You're exactly who God is looking for.

It's even a human tendency (though notably in *God's* world) to initially, repeatedly or completely overlook and reject an extraordinary purpose or ability. Let's venture into "funny" for a little lighter subject matter: The man who does the voice of Sesame Street's Elmo was told by the creators, "We like what you're doing but hate the laugh. Lose the laugh." Before he had a chance to do so, we had the Tickle Me Elmo pandemic, with parents mobbing stores to buy the doll that did nothing but laugh.

Then there's my personal favorite: After watching the pilot episode of *I Love Lucy,* the executive director of the show said, "Keep everybody but the redhead. Fire her." Putting it mildly, the redhead avoided the firing. She became the classic icon the whole world then studied as the epitome of comic talent. There's encouragement in that irony, so alongside all the Scriptures that jump to attention to deliver God's strength at pivotal moments, I'm sure the Lord doesn't mind that I now and then simply lean on the maxim "Fire the redhead."

I never thought I'd find Jesus, Lucy and Elmo on the same page. But if you're still not with me, or if you think your circumstances are too settled against you, let me share one of the most pictorial testimonies I've ever heard.

I was in a Nashville church when I heard a powerful "almost wasn't" testimony. I've heard many people's testimonies through the years about almost losing—or almost not gaining— their lives. There are stories of people cured from disease or rescued from peril, even my own story of a medically necessitated abortion that was stopped (I was blessed with a mother who took life-threatening risks to give her daughter a chance at life). But the testimony of this pastor's friend was effectively graphic, a two-seconds-closer-to-the-edge testimony of the will of God being done, no matter how bleak things look.

My weakness has often launched my greatest adventures.

It began with a group of radical pro-lifers who were on a late-night mission to collect whatever disturbing evidence they could out of a Dumpster behind a local abortion clinic. To their dismay, they found a fully intact infant body discarded amongst the rubble. It was not only a human tragedy, but biologically illegal.

They confiscated the body as confirmation of their argument against abortion, wrapping it respectfully in a cloth. Halfway home, the person who was holding the bundle noticed that it was growing warm beneath his hand. Unwrapping the cloth, he noticed very shallow, fragile breathing. The discarded infant was alive! In shock, they rushed him to the emergency room where the baby was stabilized and given a chance to live.

This "discarded baby" now sat on a stool in a southern church, a grown man, thanking God for his chance at life. I wonder if he would have worried or doubted from his own "manger" in a Dumpster, where, if he had been old enough for logic, he would've seemed to have no hope. If a baby could know the difference between hope and despair, would he hope in the improbable, like God giving silent driving directions to a car full of activists? *I have plans for him yet.*

But you and I are old enough to know. We can believe even from the bottom of our Dumpsters, as the last breath threatens to leave our bodies, that God can send a way. If we listen to His promises, we can believe His way will be perfect (see 2 Samuel 22:33).

Listen. Hope. Believe. He has plans for you yet.

Reflections

1. Do you give too much weight to your weaknesses when considering something God has asked you to do? Do you consider your weaknesses an obstacle, or do you hand them to the Lord to be used as a tool?

2. If you feel limited by your weaknesses or inadequacies, ask God to show how His strength is sufficient for any task.

Prayer

Lord, while I learn to be strong in You, help me to revel in my weakness. Don't ever let the knowledge of my own inadequacy be the tie that binds my hands when You've cut them loose long ago. Father, of course I'm un-

able. I will fear; I will fall short; I will fail and fail again. But this is not news to You; it's what You've already remedied. And to refuse You the right to come in and be my strength, my capability, simply because of my weakness and fallibility is to make two wrongs, which I know does not make a right. So keep me from saying "I can't," "I stutter," "I'm afraid." At times, Lord, I am utterly wretched, hoping that the world never sees certain failings of mine, that such things might never reflect negatively on You. But what they don't see, may You strengthen, clean, change and restore. And what they do see, may You use to show the world what You can do with even the chiefest of sinners such as I (see 1 Timothy 1:15, KJV). Amen.

16

Because He Is God

How good it is to sing praises to our God,
  how pleasant and fitting to praise him! (Psalm 147:1)

Halfway through the writing of this book, I began going through my mental list of stories that I'd collected over the years. They were my stories and others' stories, stories that had seen podiums and café tables, stories that invariably illustrated the truths of God. I searched my mind, trying to remember the ones I'd forgotten, and while doing so, what occurred to me was the importance of exploring all those truths *without* the stories.

The stories have their worth and their power, of course. They are the two-by-fours of testimony (Revelation 12:11 even states that, together with the blood of the Lamb, our testimony is what will overcome the Accuser), and they are God's joy to send to us.

The stories are there every day. There's the famous story of the man who asked God if He still speaks to people nowadays and then was moved to bring a gallon of milk to an unfamiliar house, where he discovered a distraught couple arguing over not having enough money to buy milk for their child. Or there's the story about the woman who went overseas to adopt a child, pray-

ing that God would show her "the one," and as she held the little
boy to whom her heart was drawn, she discovered that he was
wearing her son's old shoes, which she'd donated to charity
months before. His name was still written on the bottom. There
arc stories of financial needs that are suddenly met to the exact
penny, making an additional point in their exactness, and love
stories too bizarre and spread too far over time and geography to
be anything less than divine intention. Books line shelves, filled
with stories of miracles of provision, reunion and promise. It's
God's way. It's His heart.

But what if there were no stories? What if there never came
the exact, last-minute provision or the unfathomable, dramatic
miracles that seem to break open the supernatural air? What if
there were no needs sent to Him in hope of miracles? Within
our prayers, how often do we go to Him not to ask Him to carry
us a step further or to hold our loved ones and bless them, not to
heal us or help us (again, indeed His joy), but just for the sake of
His pure glory? How often do we take on the task of the cheru-
bim and let our entire enterprise be merely to call Him holy,
"Holy, holy, holy is the Lord God Almighty, who was, and is, and
is to come" (Revelation 4:8), and nothing more than that? How
often do we take the time to sit in His presence, not for our sakes
but *because* of Him, letting the light of His love sting our faces like
the perfect fire, just because He is Jesus, just because He is? If
you're as human as the rest of us, then that answer is "Not nearly
enough."

While giving due credit to the power of testimony, I want to
focus for a moment on the truths of God *without* the "oh-my-
goodness" stories. Walk with Him for just a moment onto early
golden streets. Visit His glory just for the sake of calling right
"right." You'll discover something in approaching Him in this
manner. You'll discover that the fulfillment of His glory, the finishing touch of it, His final intention of it is in you, in the ex-

change of understanding between you and your Creator. His glory is completed in what He knows you will become in Him.

To be pedantic, Hebrews describes Jesus as "the radiance of God's glory and the exact representation of his being" (1:3). Jesus describes Himself as the Light, and in Matthew 5:14 He proclaims, "You are the light of the world." In the original grammar, the form of *you* is plural here, meaning "you all," and the light remains singular. If His light—*the* Light—lives within you, and the Light is the exact representation of the glory of God, then you *are* the gospel story in action and the completion of His love. His Spirit is literally—not by our own greatness, but because of His doing—housed within you. You are His Light, the completion of His glory.

How often do we go to Him just for the sake of His pure glory?

This is, of course, a precarious discussion, as human error could tip it at any time into human arrogance, thinking He "needs" us to complete His glory. This is quite untrue; rather, the Almighty God has *chosen* to involve us. As described earlier in our exploration of true humility in the Lord being utter boldness in His presence, because He sanctioned it, the same careful balance exists here, in that we are the completion of His glory not by anything we've done, but because He's sanctioned it. It's His design, the perfection of His holiness in a given love accepted and returned to its rightful receiver. He *is* His intention of love for us.

In the beginning, when there was nothing, He knew us. And "while we were still sinners" (Romans 5:8), He knew, then, more of our hearts and more of our sin than has even been lived yet. Now, in our continued imperfection, how can we be associated at all with His glory, much less the reflection or completion of it?

It is possible because He sees His intention, the unchangeable, finished product. Even before we claim His love, He sees what we will become, standing in His presence. Because His promises are unwavering and nothing can defeat what He has begun in us, the moment we take His hand is for Him the same as the moment we stand before Him. His Word finished it long ago.

You are His Light, the completion of His glory.

Take a moment today to stare into the face of who He is, simply because of who He is. Not for what He can do for you, not for the stories He will write and has written, but because He is the Creator, even known by every creature of the earth and the air (see Revelation 5:12-14). He is the Light and the one who loves you, the one in whom every creature lives and has its being (see Revelation 4:11). He is the gentle majesty behind the beauty that enfolds you. He is the beginning and the end, Alpha and Omega (see Revelation 22:13). He is above all else, and He is to be glorified simply in His singular, perfected existence, yet He chose to make His glory *about* loving you.

Glorify the Lord. Love Him. It is the completion of His heart's greatest desire, a very divine desire.

Reflections

1. What does God's sovereignty mean to you?
2. What things most remind you that He's not only Lord of your life, but Lord of all creation?

3. How often do you praise Him simply for being Lord, for the fact that He is almighty, that He loves you? How often do you thank Him for the mere existence of Jesus, the gift of His Son? (Have you yet today?)

Prayer

Lord, not for what You can do for me—what You have done and what You've promised You will do—but because You are worthy, because You are God, I praise You. I know I cannot grasp Your magnitude, Your heart, Your presence, Your nature. I cannot grasp the hands that made the universe from nothing. But by Your gift and by Your reaching, I can know it's You. You are beyond imagination, yet realized. Trying to come only to praise You, asking nothing, my prayer would be simply, "Holy, holy, holy is the Lord God Almighty, who was, and is, and is to come" (Revelation 4:8). But one thing I ask even now: Let me always know enough to praise You. If there is nothing else, grant me enough to call You holy. Perfect Lord God, Creator, Redeemer, the beginning and the end . . . and now. Keep the stones quiet and grant me the honor of singing their song (see Luke 19:40). My Lord, my Lord, my Lord, You are holy. Amen.

17

Nothing but the Cross

For he is the living God
  and he endures forever;
 his kingdom will not be destroyed,
  his dominion will never end. (Daniel 6:26)

*T*here's a story that began on September 11, 2001, that grows more powerful with every passing day. Like many images of hope that were born on a day of destruction, this one seems to take tears and make them shine with hope. God's comfort came to prove that His love cannot pass away.

It was the third day after the attacks and a man named Frank Silecchia was moved by a view at Ground Zero that he described as "Calvary": tiny "crosses" sticking up out of the rubble everywhere. In the center of this array of cross-section I-beams was one proportionately perfect, ten-ton, eighteen-foot cross standing upright, impaled into the rubble of World Trade Center Six.

Frank's reaction to this scene was nothing less than heroic because of what it would come to mean to millions worldwide, both immediately and, Lord willing, for centuries to come. He simply responded to the cross.

Not only did he begin to draw attention to the cross's existence, spray painting "God's House" on the surrounding rubble walls; he also didn't hesitate to put the healing message of the gospel to use. He brought people to the cross so they could be renewed—renewed while standing on the ultimate site of ruin. In perfect character, God began to directly use ruination to restore. It's the nature of the Cross.

Quietly and in awe, people gathered at the site of that cross. There were workers who had seen too much, of whom too much had been asked, and still they had responded in Christlike love. There were celebrities and global figures like Benjamin Netanyahu, the former prime minister of Israel. And there was a local Franciscan priest named Brian Jordan.

God began to directly use ruination to restore. It's the nature of the Cross.

Like Frank, Father Brian saw it too, the calm and mighty proclamation in the cross and the potential it had if only its message could be clearly, globally and permanently heard. Between the two of them, Frank and Father Brian secured the right to have that cross excavated and preserved, which is a much more precarious task than you would imagine, especially at such a time as September 2001 in New York (the mayor's commission was a little too busy to be honoring special requests).

But when God moves, there's no such thing as an obstacle. (If there's an obstacle that you're facing now, especially note the tenacity of Frank and Father Brian. Don't miss the lesson of what persistence for the Lord's sake can do and to what scale.) The cross was successfully excavated and situated high atop the site at Ground

Zero so that everyone serving on that site could look up and see it. It was a scene straight out of the Old Testament, reminiscent of the bronze snake mounted on a pole so that "anyone who is bitten can look at it and live" (see Numbers 21:7-9), which later described Christ Himself: "Just as Moses lifted up the snake in the desert, so the Son of Man must be lifted up, that everyone who believes in him may have eternal life" (John 3:14-15).

Of course, there began to arise a little bit of political controversy over the cross at Ground Zero. Some asked, "How can you erect a 'religious icon' at a site where religious fanaticism caused the greatest civilian devastation in American history?" Christians responded slightly, a little sheepish and understanding of the "politically correct" side of the matter. Then suddenly there was an uproarious defense, not necessarily from Christians, but from people of all faiths who had been to Ground Zero, and especially from those who had worked at the site and *depended* on that cross to keep them going. In paraphrase, they responded, "It doesn't matter what faith you are of, and it's not about religion. When I looked up from the horror of Ground Zero and saw that cross, I saw hope and brotherhood. I saw human beings working with a strength not their own. I saw every barrier broken down and one heart begin to work within us together. I saw the ability to go on. Most of all, I saw love."

The "nonbelievers" who said these things sometimes prefaced their comments by saying, "I may not see Jesus like some do when they look at the cross, but it still matters to me because I do see hope and brotherhood, broken barriers and love." What struck me so gently as they described what they *did* see was that they were seeing Jesus. They just didn't name Him or recognize that all those things *were* Him, from Him and of Him, that all those things are ultimately inevitabilities of the cross.

But that wasn't the end of the story. I visited the cross at Ground Zero many, many times in my last year and a half in New York, and the stories of how it changed individual lives, not to mention the feeling in the air in lower Manhattan, could fill a book. One lasting illustration of the overall impact of that cross came on the one-year anniversary of 9-11.

I was at the site to do a radio interview—and so was the rest of the entire world. The winds had kicked up to violent degrees, making for an eerie day. There was a memorial being held at Ground Zero which included the reading of over 5,000 names, the names of every single person who'd been lost the previous year. The sky was as clear as it had been on the first September 11, but the added winds were grounds for all sorts of metaphor. As tons of paper and debris swirled twenty stories in the air, it seemed like the city itself was having its own memorial, the buildings that had felt the towers go down, the streets and structures of the financial district that had witnessed the horror, paying tribute in their own way.

I had been watching the scene from my television at home on Seventy-fifth Street, but now I was on-site, and the list of names of those lost was still going. After a subway ride and a long walk, an entire commute, the names were still going. I knew the cross was there, but I hadn't yet thought of it in the context of the different surroundings of the anniversary memorial with thousands and thousands gathering, encircling the area. The roads were closed, the people packed in. Though there's always a steady stream of visitors to the site, this scene was very different from visiting on any other day.

The massive number of people properly defined the size of the loss—both the loss of life and the more literal absence of mass that usually filled the sky at that spot. For anyone who never saw the towers in person, they were not simply large buildings. They were impossible structures; if you stood at the base against them, you couldn't see the edges, side to side, and could barely see the top. Their absence, to a local and physically present crowd, was a loud and piercing absence in the air. There we were, at the site that used to be the World Trade Center, two of the largest structures on earth, and every last element of their existence was gone, wiped away, scrubbed right out of the air. There was nothing but clean, empty air. There were no people on the forty-third floor because there was no forty-third floor. There were no dishes from the restaurant, no broken remnants of structure, no reminders, nothing in the sixteen-story chasm but clean, bulldozed clay. There was nothing for 110 stories up but loud, empty, bright blue air. Except . . . right there. It finally caught my eye. There at the crossroads of Trinity and Church Streets (did you catch that?) was the cross, in many more ways than one.

When there was nothing else, what remained was the cross.

High above the chasm, on a cement pillar, eighteen feet of steel with arms stretched wide promised, "I am here, I am enough, I am bigger than this story. *I am who I am*" (see Exodus 3:14). When all else had been wiped away, when destruction had come with the intent of annihilation, when "political correctness" had tried to argue and failed, when there was nothing else, what remained was the cross. Nothing but the cross.

In an era when humans would never willingly erect a cross in such a "sensitive society," God had erected *His* cross. He stamped it down as the signature to tell the end of the story: *There is hope in the deepest darkness, and it is Me. When all else has passed away, when man comes in to destroy, there is My cross and everything it means. There is all I have done for you. Though I have been repeatedly rejected and turned away, it is never taken from you. It is the only thing that will remain when all else has been done.*

Wherever you are, whatever your circumstances, no matter the odds or the anguish, He is there to stamp the iron cross of

His signature onto your personal Ground Zero—His cross, which nothing can eliminate or threaten.

As thousands through the years come to Ground Zero to remember what happened there and how we all responded, we will continue—because of one ironworker's response to Calvary and ultimately because of God's desire to heal—to gather as we did on that first anniversary, at the foot of the cross. We will be literally, metaphorically, physically, spiritually, in any manner, at the foot of the cross, where "it is finished" indeed (John 19:30).

Reflections

1. What personal Ground Zero do you want God to stamp His cross on, promising He is there and will prevail as Lord?
2. Was there a time when you lost sight of the cross and God caught your attention once again? What did He do to remind you of His sovereignty over your situation?
3. When others are in need of comfort and hope, are you willing to take them to the cross?

Prayer

Lord, remain. We do not deserve Your presence at the final hour. We do not deserve all that comes from Your hand after we have denied You, taken only the portions of Your gift that are easiest to take. But stay, Lord, and teach us how to love You and know You. Make it clear to us that You are our patient shepherd and powerful, redeeming Lord. Let us see Your cross quietly speaking victory as it stands on the hilltop, never forgetting the magnitude of what was given, what was nailed firmly to that cross. Forgive us for looking away from the cross, and thank You for turning our eyes toward it when we need it most. Thank You that when we are broken, You fill our eyes with nothing but the cross. Dear Lord, remain. Amen.

18

I Do Believe

And this is his command: to believe in the name of his Son, Jesus Christ, and to love one another as he commanded us. (1 John 3:23)

When the blind men came to Jesus in the Gospel of Matthew and cried, "Have mercy on us, Son of David," Jesus' first response was, "Do you believe I can?" (see Matthew 9:27-28).

Belief is the first step in God's formula for our salvation and one of the great enablers of the Christian faith. While it's true that God calls to our hearts first (see 1 John 4:19) and that we know Him only because He was revealed to us by our Father in heaven (see Matthew 16:17), a key element, by His design, is our belief. Notice that it was *after* the blind men had answered Jesus' launching query regarding their belief that He began to work and heal them. "[Jesus] asked them, 'Do you believe that I am able to do this?' 'Yes, Lord,' they replied. Then he touched their eyes and said, 'According to your faith will it be done to you' " (Matthew 9:28-29). It takes the adage "Seeing is believing" and turns it into God's truth: "Believing is seeing."

As we explore the spiritual impact of belief and share that belief unapologetically with others, we discover the power of being *positive*. "Positive" here does not mean "optimistic," but "sure, confident, incontestable." There is biblical promise behind the power of being *sure* of Him. It unties His hands and lets loose the fuller authority of the Holy Spirit.

If we flip through the Bible we will find many pleas for belief. The Old Testament calls God's people to believe first in Yahweh, the God of Abraham, Isaac and Jacob, and then in the Messiah to come. The New Testament calls us again to believe in the Messiah, who has become a present promise fulfilled. I couldn't begin to encapsulate the entire Scriptures' call to belief, but within only a few verses the tone is clear:

> Jesus answered, "The work of God is this: to believe in the one he has sent." (John 6:29)

> And this is his command: to believe in the name of his Son, Jesus Christ, and to love one another. (1 John 3:23)

> Therefore I tell you, whatever you ask for in prayer, believe that you have received it, and it will be yours. (Mark 11:24)

Being sure of Him unties His hands and lets loose the fuller authority of the Holy Spirit.

Why is God constantly, urgently calling for our belief? Because it is the beginning of everything He offers us and everything He is. He asserts the power of belief to overcome any obstacle, to deliver His victory over evil in any situation, to set us squarely in His hands. Belief is the power to save, not only for us but for those whose lives we will touch.

In the midst of discovering this "enabling factor," don't be discouraged or *dis*abled by your struggles with belief. Like any other element of faith, belief is not a feeling, but a decision. In Mark 9:22, a man asked Jesus to help him—"if you can." Jesus responded, " 'If you can'? . . . Everything is possible for him who believes" (9:23). Then in verse 24 we find one of the most honest statements in the Bible: "Immediately the boy's father exclaimed, 'I do believe; help me overcome my unbelief!' "

Belief and acting in accordance with it can be two very divergent things. Emotions must come second, while a choice of faith must come first. Just decide to believe. Like the man in the story above, state that you do. Don't depend on, or wait for, feeling that belief. Jesus Christ, your friend and savior, permanently fills your need beyond abundance. Just take Him at His word and believe. It's why they call it faith.

"For right now, right here, you need only to believe."

At one of the hardest junctures of my life, I hit the road to "look for" the Lord. Of course He was already at my side, but I'd let the smaller things speak to me more loudly than His constant, calm assurance, and I needed a blank road in front of me so that I could be under no influence but His. I drove to the beach and sat in my sweater in the cold, eastern spring air reading the whole book of Philippians. I had no idea at the time that it was "the book of joy," and it hadn't reached me even after I was finished reading. I was halfway there, but still at a loss as to how to go "up" from where I was at the bottom of my hill.

With a sigh I stood up and walked to the hem of my Father's ocean, and with my feet in the cold Atlantic, I said toward the horizon—but *to* something much closer—"I believe in Jesus." They were the only words I spoke out loud, but in my heart I whispered, "That's all I've got, Lord. That's the only place I know to begin."

It wasn't more than a second or two later that a goose flew from the brushes behind me on the shore, circled once around me and disappeared again into the thick Rhode Island marsh. Geese have had spiritual significance for me in the past, and as I stood there, I heard God's Spirit whispering back to me, *For right now, right here, dear child, that's all you need. You need only to believe. Now pack up your "book of joy" and walk with Me.*

Wherever you stand, speak the power of "I believe in Jesus" into it. When you don't know where to begin, you'll be amazed by the sufficiency of that statement to carry you through. Sometimes it's absolutely all you'll need. And that doesn't apply just to you; as His power changes the lives of those around you, they will be so glad you believed.

Choose today to believe.

Reflections

1. Do you believe that God is truly able to do all that you could ever ask? Whether or not He will depends on His perfect plan and sovereign knowledge, but do you believe He *can?*
2. Is there an area of your life or a precarious issue within your faith for which you need to simply take Him at His word?

Prayer

Lord, I don't always know how You're going to handle the things I encounter, the things I can't see my way out of. Sometimes I can't feel Your promises, can't sense Your delivery. But within all my frail human emotions lives a calm assurance in Your Word. Help me to remember the power of belief and show me what it means to You. When I waver, make me steadfast. When I wonder, make me sure. When I fear or tremble, help me to choose You in spite of any battling emotion. I accept Your peace, and I believe, Lord. In every way, I do. Every day, help my unbelief. Amen.

Sit Down

Sit Down

And my God will meet all your needs according to his glorious riches in Christ Jesus. (Philippians 4:19)

On the last and greatest day of the Feast, Jesus stood and said in a loud voice, "If anyone is thirsty, let him come to me and drink. Whoever believes in me, as the Scripture has said, streams of living water will flow from within him." (John 7:37-38)

When I was about eight years old my family drove to Napa Valley to spend Thanksgiving with some friends. They had a farm with sprawling vineyards and a couple of three-wheelers that were completely irresistible to an eight-year-old, especially considering the red, dusty paths and the rolling wine country that captivates one's every sense.

Before long I was riding through the vineyards of Napa Valley on the back of an ATV, holding tightly to our Swedish exchange student, and off we went, laughing and choking in the dust that was rising around us.

When we realized that we could no longer see through the dust well enough to drive, we slowed to a stop. Laughing still and waiting for the sunlit dust to clear, we had no idea that we were in the middle of a mild miracle. As the dust cloud dissipated, we noticed that not even inches away, but directly *over* our front wheel, was a taut silver vine cable. Had we stopped a half-second later, we would have been tossed at full speed from the ATV. We slowly backed the wheel out from under the cable, counting our blessings and our limbs. I think we were more relieved that we wouldn't be in trouble with the grown-ups than by the fact that we had avoided serious injury.

I was only a child at the time and not attentive to "devotional living"—seeking God's lessons in any moment or through any illustration. I wasn't watching for His hand in my life or listening to His voice to learn as I walked with Him, so at the time I didn't take the incident for any more than an almost disastrous near miss. Then, as I began to tell this story to a friend twenty years later, the now-developed habits of recognition began to reveal the story for what it really was.

God allows us to be blinded to get us seated so we won't miss His miracle, His work, His intention.

The first thing that can be learned is that God's hand is there to withhold us from danger, to stop or to redirect us. We often aren't even aware of His direction and are simply reacting to a circumstance that seems to be entirely unrelated. In other words, God directs our paths more often by arranging our circumstances than by saying flat-out, *Don't go down that road; there's danger there.* For instance, most of the "avoidance" stories from 9-11 involve broken-down cars, sore throats or trouble with alarm clocks that kept people home from work that day. Very few, if any, involve God saying to a person's spirit, *Don't go in to work today.* Perhaps God leads us in such a way because He knows that we might not listen to Him if we can "logic away" His guidance. We might not believe that what we're hearing is His voice, or we might not properly respond to what He tells us. So, nowadays, when it really counts He simply stops us with His hand rather than with His voice.

There are reasons God does this, sometimes blinding us purposefully, just as my friend and I were blinded by the dust. One reason is so that we can learn to trust Him and be secure in our knowledge of His voice and the assurance of His spirit—which we'll get into further in a few pages. But another reason God allows us to be blinded is to get us to stop and focus. Just as the dust stopped us right in the nick of time and then cleared to reveal a hazard I hadn't even considered at the time, so God allows us to be blinded to get us seated and rapt so we won't miss His miracle, His work, His intention. That moment "under the wire" was an opportunity to realize, "God is watching my path." Not only watching, protecting and guiding, but all along wanting me to *know* that He is. He takes these opportunities to sharpen our awareness of our relationship with Him, or to reveal it for the first time, depending on where you are on your walk with Him.

Nowhere is our need to sit down and pay attention more literally, succinctly and yet inconspicuously illustrated than in the story of the loaves and the fishes (Matthew 14:13-21; Mark 6:30-44; Luke 9:10-17; John 6:1-15). We may think the big lesson there is that Jesus can multiply fish and bread. Now, I'm not undercutting that miracle; it is one of the most prominent in the Bible. I'm just saying that there were even larger lessons hidden within the whole experience. For example, the entire gospel story, from start to finish, is represented, hidden within this story as Christ receives the gift from heaven, gives thanks, breaks it into pieces, gives the bread to His disciples and says, in essence, "Feed my sheep." And when they had done so all who had eaten were satisfied, and there were twelve basketfuls left over to feed the ones who had fed the people.

Let's look at just one illustration that shows how God was already teaching in an understated but almost more powerful way before the actual miracle even took place. It began with the typical human flaw of not comprehending Christ as the fulfillment of any need, no matter what. The disciples looked at their situation and saw a remote and desolate area that clearly could not provide the necessary sustenance for all those people. Problem number one is that they looked at their circumstances rather than at Christ in expectation. He even tried to get them to adjust their thinking after they presented the problem: He replied, *"You* give them something to eat" (Matthew 14:16; Mark 6:37; Luke 9:13). Still they saw only a lack. So God began to make His sufficiency large enough for all to see— and we can still see it 2,000 years down the road.

But how? He didn't find a high place and announce, "Everyone pay attention. Miracle coming." He didn't implore the crowd to expect a life-changing moment as their reason to turn to Him. He told them simply to sit down. " 'Have them sit down in groups of about fifty each.' The disciples did so, and everybody sat down" (Luke 9:14-15). The sitting is an inadvertent act of faith. Look no further. In any expectation, any need or lack, even when you are filled and simply curious or desirous to know more of God—whatever your surroundings, whatever "it" is, sit down and look to the One standing in your midst.

Oh, that we could get past the point of asserting, like the disciples, "But, Lord, I can see there's no provision here." Rather, may our first response be to sit down and look to God in expectation. "Lord, I have followed You here. I look to You, regardless of what my surroundings seem. I need nothing more than what comes from Your hands." We will find our needs met in ways we couldn't have imagined or requested, and, in His way, He will meet them in abundance.

Perhaps now is a moment to sit down and watch Him expectantly, not only for your sake, but for His, because it is His joy when you trust His ability and desire to be your complete provision. Even when your immediate surroundings look unpromising, no matter how far you are from where you think you need to be or how desolate the day, Christ is there and He is able.

No matter how far you are from where you think you need to be, Christ is there and He is able.

If you find yourself squeezing the work of a thousand into one thinly spread life (kind of the reverse of the loaves and fishes miracle), remember His unchanging formula and do all you do as unto the Lord. In the rush of every day, tell Him, "I look to You alone to provide, even in this remote place." Catch a glimpse of His eyes and see where He points you next. It may be He will send you in a very unlikely direction. It may be He will say, "Sit down. Stand still. Be still in the core of your heart."

My advice: Do what He says. He is Christ the King, and He knows what's coming next.

Reflections

1. When you are in the company of the Messiah, what are some of the ways you still look elsewhere for what you need?
2. When you're worried about a certain lack, how difficult is it for you to follow Jesus to a remote place and sit down?
3. Is there a provision you're in need of right now, and how much are you looking to the One in your midst to provide for you?

Prayer

Lord, help me to expect You to be my provision in every moment, no matter what my surroundings or my need. Let it be my first and only instinct to sit down and look to You, waiting for whatever You will do. When You speak, may I be prepared at all times to respond accordingly. If You tell me to sit down when I'm bent on searching out an answer to my problems, catch my attention and tell me again to simply sit down in Your presence. I know You are the maker of miracles, Jesus. I will never be able to know all that You do, to know what's coming next, but I do know this: You are all I will ever need, and if I follow where You lead, I need never look elsewhere. It is my joy to wait for what You will do. Amen.

20

Walking by
the Sound of
His Voice

But the Counselor, the Holy Spirit, whom the Father will send in my name, will teach you all things and will remind you of everything I have said to you. (John 14:26)

In the last few pages, we covered one constructive function of earthly "blindness": getting us to sit down and focus on God. We also mentioned that another purpose of our human blindness is to teach us to be secure in our knowledge of God's voice and the assurance of His Spirit. There is great freedom and intimacy in learning to walk only by the sound of His voice and nothing else, in learning the infallibility of "because He says so" and leaning fully into it.

Brennan Manning shares a revealing illustration in his book *Ruthless Trust: The Ragamuffin's Path to God* regarding the difference between trust and clarity. The illustration begins with a conversation between John Kavanaugh and Mother Teresa in which Kavanaugh asks Mother Teresa for her prayers that he would find clarity. She refuses, in essence saying that she's never had clarity; what she's had is trust, and that's what she would pray for on his behalf. Manning writes, "Craving clarity, we attempt to eliminate the risk of trusting God. Fear of the unknown path stretching ahead destroys childlike trust in the Father's active goodness and unrestricted love."[1]

The picture this illustration prompted in my own spirit left me calmer, more excited about the unknown and with several fewer questions for God. It left me enjoying the trade-off of my blinded, earthbound eyes for the privilege of walking sure of Him.

Imagine the path, and the usual accompanying request: "Show me the way I should go. Light my way." There's nothing faulty in this request. There is a season for it, as there is for all things. His Word is even called "a lamp to my feet and a light for my path" (Psalm 119:105). But imagine the relief and the relationship of not *needing* to know the way. There are seasons when God will not show us what's just down the path, for good reason, whether it's because we're not meant to know or, greater than that, so that we'll simply look to Him in that perfect willingness of trust. It's a beautiful exchange, a privilege.

Why do the sheep know the shepherd's voice?
Because they've heard it before.

A small portion of this blind trust is captured in Jesus' own words in John 20:29: "Then Jesus told him, 'Because you have seen me, you have believed; blessed are those who have not seen and yet have believed.' " Even the angels don't have the chance to realize the love, the completion of the whole desire in the words "I trust You, God. *Because* of You, I trust You." I can almost imagine God in great exhale. We have heard His voice, we have recognized Him, and the message, long given, has at last been understood and accepted.

But this is not an "it is finished" (John 19:30) moment; this is the beginning. This is where we find the comfort of our own feet on the path and aren't swayed in the slightest if we can't see our hands in front of our faces. When our petition changes from "Show me, Lord" to "None of it matters if I'm fully in Your hands, on Your path, in Your sight. I trust You," that's when we really begin to go.

If we listen very carefully, we'll find that He gives us repeated opportunities, when we're ready, to practice this skill—and it does take practice. Why do the sheep know the shepherd's voice? Because they've heard it before. According to the Lord, in the literal, spiritual application of it, the sheep know His voice because *He* knows *them* (see John 10:27).

A greater privilege that comes from knowing His voice and responding to it is when He allows us to reach others' hearts in a way that only His Spirit would know how to do, at a time only His Spirit could know is perfect. I've witnessed this privilege over the years as I've watched others unwittingly change and comfort the lives of those around them through their responses to God's leading, their trust in His wisdom and accuracy.

I also remember the first time *I* fully appreciated the nudge of the Holy Spirit in regard to someone else's need. It was not the most powerful of experiences, but it was the most important, because it was where I first acknowledged the constant activity of the spiritual realm around me, beside me, within me, at all times—and acknowledged that I'd been disregarding it my whole life.

I sat in a real estate office watching a woman having a dreadful day and passing it on to everyone around her—on the phone, in the office. There were two men literally "hiding" against the back wall of the room, sharing a desk so as to steer clear of trouble. I watched as the woman lit cigarette off of cigarette—with two or three of them going at once in the ashtray—slammed phones and papers, barked and finally gave up, taking two of her latest cigarettes outside. She was not happy.

It would usually be my style to run to the aid of those she'd mowed down, not to her. But as I sat there thinking, "Sheesh,

New Yorkers," I heard crying outside. She was crying? It would be simple for me to go out with intentions of comfort, but something else happened. I sensed, for the first time *ever* in my life, the Lord saying, *Go and tell her about Me.*

Again, this was back in a time of my life when "Holy Spirit" was not in my vocabulary. I still thought that randomly telling someone Jesus loved her would peg me a daisy-toting hippie, a goodie-two-shoes, a "Jesus freak," and I simply had more manners than that. My method was to mind my own business, be seen and not heard and remain politically correct. My faith was more "sophisticated" than all that.

It feels like a miracle to know His voice.

The God in whom I believed had said in the Scriptures, "Go and tell the world" (see Matthew 28:19), and there I was reading those words on the page of my day as if I'd never really considered them. There was a difference, too, between the general command and the request when it was specific to a circumstance. He didn't just say, *Go tell the world* in principle. He said, *Go tell her.*

I spent what felt like a half-hour gripping the edge of a threadbare sofa, telling God it just wasn't in me, not here, not now. "You saw her, Lord. She'll kill me, have me arrested. I'd have to run!" But somehow I got up and out the door, gritted my teeth and squeezed "Jesus" out between them.

To my surprise, the woman burst into a tearful story about her mother passing away and a Bible her mother had always tried to give her, which she'd just found as she was sorting through her mother's effects. She said that she needed to know more than anything that it wasn't too late. Her mother had been the only one who sent her

"Jesus-ward," and with her gone the woman wondered if Jesus was still there, and if He was, did He still want her?

It's important to note that sometimes it *is* enough to simply comfort. But this particular situation was about God's front-burner intentions for the moment—both to meet the woman's need of Him and my need to learn how to speak up and to watch where my Father is working and follow (see John 5:17).

This leaves us with this question: After we're ready and able to listen, are we willing then to follow? Both call for practice. We must practice listening in order to be further able to recognize when it's He versus other competing voices. We should practice listening in order to recognize His voice sooner so we'll be able to meet the unknown needs around us, in the moment, responding to the supernatural. And we must listen, simply out of love, beyond all the other reasons, just because we want to know His voice, which provides comfort like that which we find in the familiar voices of our loved ones on earth, but is so unfathomably multiplied.

It feels like a miracle to know His voice, the voice that comforts the waves of the sea. Hear the Shepherd calling. Listen, know and go to Him. Go *with* Him, wherever He is going

Reflections

1. Is there something you feel God is asking you to do that you're afraid to act on?

2. Do you recognize His voice? Can you remember the last time (or any time) that you sensed Him speaking His love to you, individually? His direction? His comfort?

3. Ask the Lord to show you how to hear Him more clearly, how to know His caring, shepherding, sovereign voice.

Prayer

Jesus, trust can sometimes look like a tall order from where I stand, but only because I am viewing it from within the limited bounds of my human understanding. Trusting You is such a simple request, if I would just remember who You are. So teach me, Lord. Make me not only completely comfortable with my eyes closed to the path ahead, but downright excited, knowing the character and capability of the One who holds my hand. Let me be so taken just with the honor of traveling this road with You that nothing of what I cannot see concerns me. Plant my feet on Your road, Lord, but keep my eyes only excitedly on Yours. Amen.

Note

1. Brennan Manning, *Ruthless Trust: The Ragamuffin's Path to God* (San Francisco: HarperSanFrancisco, 2000), n.p.

21

Little Shoots

But he knows the way that I take;
when he has tested me, I will come forth as gold. (Job 23:10)

I am once again at a borrowed house in the country, here to sit uninterrupted and seek the Lord for the sake of these pages. I couldn't be in a more ideal place, both for my personal tastes and for observing the handiwork and constant activity of the Lord. Here I can watch the puzzle of nature being put together progressively from dawn to dusk and then starting again as dawn returns. I can see the sparrows being cared for not just in theory but in reality. I can see the joy of the Lord in what He's created and in how He works it all together around me.

From where I sit on a wide, red deck I can see just about every bird ever made. There's a redheaded black woodpecker keeping watch from a hole in a tree, which I can only assume by its behavior has babies in it. Geese of every goose-color come and go all day on their landing strip of river. There are doves and magpies and early robins. There are horses on both sides of the water, unconventionally playful, and an excitable dog complaining to them over the fence. I even caught a silkworm riding its string down to the edge of my knee.

But as I sat here watching the birds, thinking that they were my lesson for the day (God's care for every sparrow, the beauty in the colors they wear), I began to study even more intently the trees that were their stages, and it was there that I found my lesson. God was in the mood for Sunday school, and as usual He'd brought along a beautiful storyboard.

The trees of northern California, oak or birch or walnut, are dramatic most of the time; they are gnarled, stocky, contoured and configured in beautiful forms and constantly expanding in different directions. One walnut tree even grew up *through* the deck directly beside me. Growing precariously straight outward from the side of its trunk are little shoots of all sizes. A few are just sprouts of new leaves that could be felled by a single raindrop; others are stems still too fragile for the smallest bird's perch. Directly above me, however, are a line of five or six shoots that are well on their way to achieving stability as bona fide limbs.

Remember what a gift it is to come to Him just as you are.

No bigger around than a number two pencil, they seem so out of place sporadically stuck to the side of a huge walnut trunk, such a contrast in size. I could snap them off with little effort. And then barely two feet above them is a limb that could be a couple of decades old, a limb that would easily bear all of my weight. The difference between the immature and the full-grown limbs is emphasized by their proximity to one another.

I have been the little shoot in far too many scenarios, not only "back in my beginnings" (see Hebrews 5:12) but repeatedly as I climb and fall throughout my journey, learning the same things constantly. And yet I have longed to be the stronger limb, not only strong enough to be less at risk, but to support the weight of others as they climb and consider the work of His hands.

"Make me the sturdy limb," I asked of God. I know He has done so at times and that He will continue to do so in more ways as I grow. But that day God gave me a key response to my request: *Not only did the sturdy limb begin as a little shoot, but it* had *to begin that way.* There is no instant tree. There is no limb which, because of its "exceptional quality" begins to grow fatly from the side of the trunk. All limbs start as little shoots. All trunks need every ring they've got, every ring they've earned.

The above, which may even be cliché, was just enough to get me focused on the concept God knew I needed to learn that day, but it was only the beginning of my understanding of this truth, which was then followed by an endless stream of illustrations and analogies.

For example, just as parents in the delivery room are not disappointed with the infant who is unable to immediately say his alphabet or drive a car, so God is all the more aware of where we are on our journeys to becoming strong branches in His kingdom. Don't assume your weakness (which we explored earlier) means that you're not slated to be the sturdy limb. Don't look at the picture you see of yourself and decide accordingly what God will use you for, what your place is in the unfolding daily puzzle. His picture is the completed version; He reads the story backwards, end first, knowing who you will become, the choices you will make when He gives you a second chance—or a third. This is not an excuse for limiting your aims or dragging your feet, for just as the infant begins to grow and expectations for his development change, so God is calling upon you to reach for His hand to pull you up to the next plateau. But don't let "you" stop you.

In a biology book long gone, I read about a butterfly who'd been "helped" out of its cocoon by a well-meaning nurturer. Much to that nurturer's dismay, he discovered that he'd disrupted a perfectly designed process that was intended to strengthen the butterfly's wings—a tissue-thin cape of arms that

built their strength through the adversity of transformation so
that they would be ready at the moment of freedom to fly. Without this "exercise," this period of struggle and "inability," the
wings would never find their strength and the butterfly would
never achieve the identity that God was waiting to bestow.

On the road to becoming a greater person in Christ, remember what a gift it is to come to Him just as you are and to build
strength through your struggles. Be prepared to be stretched and
challenged, rained on and perched on. Expect to fight to hold on
to your Source. Be prepared and remain prepared, for there is
never a final arrival that deems us completely invincible, at least
not while we're here on earth. As a sturdy limb can do nothing
without the trunk, so the branch can do nothing without the vine
(see John 15:5). You are fellable without Him, no matter how far
it seems you've come.

I made the Lord an odd promise on New Year's Day this year.
I prayed, "I will not vow to be the person I am not yet ready to
become." Under normal circumstances, I would have considered this a defeatist attitude, shooting shorter than the stars. But
I was discovering what a great division of grace it is to give oneself
wholly, realistically and fearlessly to God. There is a boldness in
it, an acceptance of the sufficiency of what Christ has done and a
sharp defiance of the lies Satan tells of all the reasons we should
shrink from grace and glory (see Hebrews 10:39).

There, in that confession of limitation, a firm foundation took
root. It wasn't the resolution's objective that mattered; rather, it
was the simplicity it unearthed, the recognition that wherever I
am in my walk with God, as long as my hand is in His, I'm where
I should be. Christ knows who I am and who I will become. He's
authored it. He's finished it. He saw my full worth under the
light of His redemption and He paid the full price.

There's a true story of a man who was a woodworker by trade,
struggling and in debt, who saw his neighbor throwing out a

grand, old wooden chair. It was fine craftsmanship, only a little old and worn, and would be so easy to restore—in the right hands. The woodworker stopped his neighbor seconds before the chair hit the Dumpster and asked, "If you're not going to use that, may I have it?"

The neighbor considered him for a moment and then without explanation said, "No."

The woodworker watched the chair smash against the edge of the Dumpster. He felt heartbroken and confused as he saw something of beauty and vital worth being destroyed for no good reason.

Years later, the man had hit even harder times and found himself at road's end. He cried out to God, asking for any good reason not to take his life. The story of the wooden chair came back to him, and he saw the image of it shattering to pieces as he heard God's desperately loving voice cry out, *If you're not going to use it, may I have it?*

I have watched God become everything.

It is in some of the deepest valleys that we may find the most accurate and enabled understanding of the human estate. In such moments of sinking to become nothing I have watched God become everything. It's a priceless comfort to be reminded of His lordship, that the One who is everything is the One who holds me—and He holds on to me by choice.

No matter where you are, there is God, who also calls Himself friend (see John 15:15) and brother, asking for you to come to the throne unashamedly and passionately, with boldness of faith, just as you are. He longs for you to be familiar and confident, sure of the gospel and the gift won willingly on the cross. Embrace it.

Perhaps the comfort and security of a sturdy limb is an image left over from childhood. I used to sit in the long, sideways limbs of an almond tree, holding fast to the strong wood below me, laying my head against the bark. I knew what I wanted to be: His. And I wanted to do well at it. I've still got a long way to go, but I'm in my place, in His hands, where He builds my limbs, asking me simple questions—such patient exhortations, touching invitations—*Do you love Me? Come, follow Me. Feed My sheep. Just believe.* Every day I grow another ring as He builds a stronger limb.

Reflections

1. What is one area of your life in which you long to be stronger? Have you brought this struggle to the Lord? What is one active thing you can do to work toward strengthening that area?
2. In what ways have you seen your walk with God change and grow over the last year? In what areas of your life is He working most strongly with you now?

Prayer

Lord, I only know who I am, not who I will become, and I'm discouraged. I long to be a greater person in Christ. I long to be something finished, unshakable, never felled. But let me not forget what a great part of the gift is in the imperfect being made perfect by Your hand. Suddenly, it is an honor to be incomplete when what completes me is You. I am willing to be built, Lord. I am willing to be patient with my smallness, even comfortable with it, as I sit in the palms of the same God who fashioned the stars from less than me. I look at the world You created from absolutely nothing— just the perfection of Your thought—and I wonder what You might be willing to create from me. Whatever I must do, Lord, to become Your clay, help me to do, that I may be something of Your imagination. Amen.

22

A Bible-Sized Faith

Is anything too hard for the LORD? (Genesis 18:14)

W hatever happened to the sun standing still (see Joshua 10:12-13)?

Yes, we're living under a new, completed covenant of love under which God's Spirit lives among us, and perhaps there are things we don't need anymore, like burning bushes and literal handwriting on the wall (see Daniel 5:5-28). But we could still use a little manna from heaven from time to time (see Exodus 16), a parting sea now and then (see Exodus 14:13-31) or perhaps a figure to stand with us in the fire and keep us from being consumed (see Daniel 3:25).

I can't remember who said this first, but I've heard it said throughout the years that "perhaps we would start seeing Bible-sized miracles in our world today if we started living like the people in the Bible." This isn't a commentary on modern-day misbehavior. That's certainly an issue, but it's a different conversation than I'd like to have here. This conversation is about building arks when there's no sign of rain, picking up our tents and walking our families into the desert if we must (see Genesis

12:1) and going into the King's court unsummoned, claiming, "If I perish, I perish" (Esther 4:16).

This is about living much bigger than most of us are used to, about being the people God created and called us to be. God is dynamic. "Big and dramatic" as my dear friend Stace often says. Just look at what He has created to get a glimpse of His ways, His character, His "decorating style"—the dramatic beauty of nature, the quietness of the breath of life. Perhaps the song has desensitized us to the depth of these words, but "our God is an *awesome* God."[1] He is not reticent with His majesty, even when using the weakest as the strongest, like He used the quiet entry of His Son into this world as an infant in a stable to bring salvation to all who would accept it. Our God is not a little God, but sometimes our prayers and our faith are both so very small.

There are stories coming in off the mission field that are so extreme at times that I'm tempted not to believe them—but then I begin speaking to people who were there. There was the woman who needed a hot-water bottle to keep a premature baby alive after its mother died giving birth, also leaving an older child behind. When the missionary was praying with some of the children of the village for God to somehow take care of the infant even though they didn't have a hot-water bottle, one child responded, "Then we must pray for a water bottle." The missionary hesitated, because they were in a tropical climate where no one would be sending a hot-water bottle, and after all, she was trying to teach these kids that faith in God *works,* not get their hopes up over what would never happen. (This is the irony by which we live.) But before the missionary could stop her, the child prayed out loud for not only a hot-water bottle "to save the baby," but also for a doll for the baby's sibling, "so she could know You love her too." Ruefully, the missionary carried the prayer in her heart, preparing to face the children's questions when it wasn't answered.

Later that day they received the first package they had gotten in four months. It was a box from the United States filled with all sorts of supplies, including a doll thrown in on top—and at the very bottom, a hot-water bottle that someone had sent, with no good reason, to a missionary in the tropics. She could have filled the hot-water bottle with her tears of joy.

Another favorite story of mine, because it brings a literal Scripture to contemporary (though third-world) life is about the man who ate poison and lived. There was a native man who responded to the gospel shared by a local missionary—a doctor, by the way, with a miracle testimony of his own—and who in turn tried to tell his village about Jesus Christ. His brothers beat and banished him. He came back and tried again. The whole village beat and banished him. He came crawling back time and time again, eager to get the "remedy" of salvation to the people he loved. Finally, when they knew that in his tenacity he would never give up, never be beaten down, they decided to kill him. Against his knowledge, they poisoned his food and called him to eat with them.

How many times would you crawl back to your village?

Thinking he had finally broken through, he ate enthusiastically and continued in every breath to share God's love with all of them. They watched, angry, as he continued to eat and not be felled. One of his zealous brothers, thinking the poison had somehow not made it into the food, reached over and took a mouthful for himself. With one bite, he died. The village had been shown, so they might believe, the might of God.

This story is not found in the Old Testament. It may have happened around a fire in a third-world country, in Old Testament style, but this took place now, in our day. Yet we can barely bring up the "sensitive" issues of Jesus in the workplace or as our loved ones lay dying. It takes such a struggle on our part, when sharing the gospel is practically a breeze for us compared to what the disciples endured, or Moses, or the man mentioned above. How many times would you crawl back to your village?

Ask yourself the question anew: How big are you believing? How big is your God? Have you made Him the size that you see Him, or are you open to Him showing you the size He actually is? Are you serving God as an element of religion, or are you serving God who is in and of Himself the great I AM, creator of the universe, Ha Shem?

Believe bigger. Leaps of faith are what start covenants moving.

These questions aren't pointed accusations; they're intended as inspiration for you to both leap into Bible-sized adventures of His limitless imagination and to rest in the hands of a God who stopped the sun in the sky, who split oceans with His thoughts, who sent angels to break chains, who led a nation with a pillar of fire and yet who pulled His glory into the form of a man and took on the debilitating body of flesh just to draw near to us. This is a God who, as a man and as God, "had compassion on the multitudes" (see Matthew 9:36; 15:32; Mark 6:34).

Believe bigger. Leaps of faith are what start covenants moving. Walk into the desert if that's the journey. Or walk into the sea, if that's the journey. But walk with Him. Walk into Bethlehem and believe the Messiah has come. Walk to Calvary and weep with all the disciples—but believe He will rise again. Walk into your own home with the efforts of peace and commitment and put Jesus at the helm. He will send manna from the skies; He will set your feet upon the water; He will be your joy in all circumstances if you ask Him to be. But, most of all, He will be with you. It's an eternal hand that holds you, the hand that held the pieces of the stars before they were stars. And you, in His hands, have far greater purpose than the stars.

If you can move a mountain with a mustard seed (see Matthew 17:20), imagine the foundations that will rumble if you stand firmly on all the promises of God. He calls you to a mighty faith. Respond.

Reflections

1. Is there someone whom you feel God is prompting you to tell about Him? Is there a specific message you're afraid to share with someone?

2. Is there something you feel prompted to do that feels too big to attempt? What scares you the most about taking a leap of faith?

3. What leap has come up in your life that is the hardest you could imagine taking?

Prayer

Never, Lord, never let me underestimate the power of what You are prepared to do. My prayers are often far too small, my willingness limited. Let me begin living a Bible-sized faith where, truly, nothing is impossible. I say I believe that anything I can imagine is possible in You. But what about what I haven't imagined? What about the sea parting and the sun standing still? Don't let my limited belief ever stand in the way of Your willingness to bestow a magnificent presence upon this earth. I know You can take nothing and make it everything. The Israelites doubted, feared and turned away from You in the desert, but even still You gave them a pillar of cloud and fire. You raised waters above their heads and rained food from Your hand. Lord, forgive us now our same volume of doubt, fear and frequent turning. Grant us the sea split in two. Grant us the size and glory of You. Almighty Ha Shem, come and reign over Your people, as You already do, but be greatly seen, Lord. Open the heavens and show us Your glory again. Amen.

Note

1. Rich Mullins, "Awesome God," *Songs*, Reunion Records, 1996.

23

Waiting
and Seeking

Yet the LORD longs to be gracious to you;
  he rises to show you compassion. . . .
  Blessed are all who wait for him! (Isaiah 30:18)

*W*aiting and seeking are often two of the most difficult
and underpracticed of skills. Perhaps there's a con-
nection there between difficulty and underpracticing. I'll grant this.
Waiting and seeking would seem to be such easy things to do compared to an active skill or assignment that you would think they
wouldn't need much practice. How hard can it be to wait, weighed
against some of our more difficult callings of service? How weak can
our seeking skills really be when, ideally, it should be what we're doing every moment of every day? Could we really be that far from
what, in our opinion, we're essentially always doing?

The sum of all these questions is this: Are we seeking to the
degree God calls us to seek Him, or do we just stick a thermome-
ter in the water and check it whenever we remember? And, as we
seek Him, how willing are we, *really,* to wait—without whining
or wondering what's taking Him so long?

During the time that I was in New York, I knew that eventually I
would return home to California. It was part of the plan (I hoped),

and I dreamed of that day as a somewhat inconceivable blessing. Ten years were committed to a place to which I believed I was "called" and therefore couldn't (wouldn't) leave until given the spiritual go-ahead. I was honored to be in the center of His will, ultimately satisfied with it, but I viewed my return home as a descent of sorts into the Promised Land. So when that day finally came, I expected a "too good to be true" peak. I was going home at last.

I drove cross-country with my mother for two solid weeks (yes, we still love one another) in a car from the Brooklyn Auto Auction. We crossed the bridge into Needles, California, with camera flashing and heart pounding, and I rolled the last leg into my hometown of Sacramento ten years older than when I'd left. I unpacked my well-traveled car, and that's when it arrived: an utter, inexplicable despair. I had expected to miss my life in the city to a degree and to go through an understandable transition period. But this was something other than that, something strange and a little frightening.

Come, like the wise men, for no greater reason than simply "Jesus is here."

Only days later, I was back in NYC on business, and being there confirmed that it wasn't "lack of city" that had fallen on my heart. "So what is it, Lord?" As I stood staring down into Forty-second Street from a twentieth-story window, He finally settled into my heart, ready to help me understand. I realized that for the first time in my life, He hadn't handed me my next step. I didn't have a direct assignment, a task, a calling I could step into immediately. I knew where I was going in general, but "now" was a different story. My whole task now was to wait, to seek and to be willing to sit quietly in His presence, unknowing, until, in His sovereignty, He was ready to divulge the next step.

I'd always been pretty good at "doing"—the big things, that is. Even when it's not my prime choice, like moving to New York, when He says, *Go,* I usually go. I may cry, whine, wish, mope or furrow, but I go. But waiting? Seeking? I am woefully inept. They are such important talents that I've yet to hone, and now they were the entirety of my job. The Lord said, *Wait for Me. Seek Me not just within the outline of an assignment or for directions on your path. For a moment, just seek Me because you see Me as worthy to be sought. Come, like the wise men, for no greater reason than simply "Jesus is here."*

Wait for Me. Seek Me.

Waiting and seeking are not necessarily sedentary (inactive) undertakings. Quite the contrary, it is sometimes during a period of waiting and seeking that we can be most beset with "life" vying for our time and attention, even tying up and bending our emotions. There may even be a specifically intended spiritual battle trying to deter us from the tasks God has given us.

Waiting and seeking are bold and active attitudes, often requiring the willingness to leap, to hope against hope (see Romans 4:18), to be prepared to believe, if only because of His word, that if He says, *Walk,* we can and perhaps must take that impossible step and expect the road to "rise up to meet us."

Waiting and seeking are not only crucial landmarks in ministry and relationship with God, but a constant entreaty throughout His Word. They are a secret of intimacy with Him. They are the beginning of any "next degree" of discovery of Him:

Be still, and know that I am God. (Psalm 46:10)

Blessed is the man who listens to me,
    watching daily at my doors,
    waiting at my doorway. (Proverbs 8:34)

Seek and you will find. (Matthew 7:7)

Jesus Himself set the example by going off alone to pray several times a day. If you train your eyes on Him, He will lead you with a glance "to the right or to the left" (Isaiah 30:21). What perfect security and privilege! Embrace the act of waiting and seeking not just as a precursor to blessing, but as the fulfillment of the blessing itself.

Are you willing and able to wait upon His Word, to wait with Him, for Him? Will you be prepared to respond? Is your trust of Him so complete that if your task is to sit quietly and watch for Him, you will do so, knowing that there's no closer you could be, in that moment, to the center of His heart, His perfect will?

Be willing to settle your heart into stillness with Him. Wait, because there is no waiting for "nothing"; He *will* lead you. And seek, because there is no seeking in vain; He *will* be found.

Reflections

1. Would you consider yourself to be patient or anxious about God's work in your life? How long are you willing to wait to see the fruition of His plan?
2. Is there something for which you've stopped praying because so much time has passed? What can you do in the meantime to show Him that He is your hope?

Prayer

Father, help me to remember the simple privilege of seeking You, of waiting at Your feet for what You will say, the great anticipation of where You will be going and the honor of going with You. Shaking off all anxiousness, handing You my doubts, I exhale and ask for calm to drink in Your Spirit. I need nothing else but to seek first Your presence. Wherever we go next, Lord, I am so glad to be here, with You. Amen.

24

What God Can Do with Dirt

This then is how we know that we belong to the truth, and how we set our hearts at rest in his presence whenever our hearts condemn us. For God is greater than our hearts, and he knows everything. (1 John 3:19-20)

Search me, O God, and know my heart;
*   test me and know my anxious thoughts.*
See if there is any offensive way in me,
*   and lead me in the way everlasting. (Psalm 139:23-24)*

*I*n the midst of one of my greatest failures I discovered a deep need I hadn't known I'd lost, and I vowed never to lose sight of it again. My gratitude for God's intimate counsel had gradually developed into an eagerness to show Him how much I was learning. With one foot out of the nest, I gathered His gifts of strength about me and tried to delight Him with my independence. But there's a crucial difference between spiritual maturity and total autonomy. I hadn't noticed I was trying to make Him proud by showing Him I needed Him less.

That's precisely when I fell, and fell hard. From within the depths of my failure I learned the measure of my unwavering, present need of Jesus Christ. I already knew that I could do nothing apart from Him (see John 15:5). It was the degree of my weakness and dangerous fallibility that caught me off guard. It shouldn't have caught me so off guard, however, because He tried to warn me.

Before the great avalanche of my foolishness, I awoke one morning to a sermon on television about temptation. It was one I'd heard before, so I knew what was coming and how purely it matched my circumstances. The pastor was speaking with first-person certainty, an "I have seen it myself" tone of experience, as he encouraged his listeners to avoid temptation entirely. Not to walk the fine wire, but to run in the opposite direction, far and fast, period. I smiled. The Lord was providing a way out (see 1 Corinthians 10:13).

His way out wasn't a forceful hand dragging me into obedience. It was only a gentle reminder of the straightest path and an invitation to walk it with Him. But how often His loving gestures—not to mention His sovereignty—are taken for granted. I saw that He was giving me a way out and I wanted to take it, but I didn't have the guts. It wouldn't have been so hard, really, but temptation is powerfully deceiving. Not only did I feel from within my circumstances that God's call to "complete avoidance" was too difficult; I also decided it was unnecessary, because I thought I could handle the temptation on my own just fine.

I grabbed the remote control, as if I could quiet the Holy Spirit, but He held out His hand an inch further when a commercial came on. It was just a network commercial for the fall lineup, but it kept playing a single lyric repeatedly: "Who do y'love, child? Come 'n' walk with me." It was one last shot to follow Him. *Decide who you love*, He was calling. *If you love Me, take My hand and walk with Me today . . . My way.* I wasn't telling Him no, but I was convinced I'd be OK, not vulnerable to temptation, at least not so much as to fall. He was trying to tell me that He knew better, that He knew I couldn't handle it my way, that I needed to trust Him and walk with Him, but I didn't listen.

"I love *You,* Lord," I whispered as I turned the television off and left for the day. But a whisper wasn't enough to keep me from falling. Bigger choices should have been made. Fighting temptation entirely like the sermon said, taking His way out, had looked so difficult from where I stood, but looking back, I can see that His hand was so present and so strong; all I had to do was take hold of it.

What about when your past is your present?

When the worst of my mistake was over, I found myself at a seminar, listening to the speaker map out a timeline of God's grace in her life. She highlighted regrettable failures in her past, revealing everything to her audience. I applauded her candor, but the timeline seemed to suggest that the "new woman" she'd become was incapable of falling to the same temptations as before, at least not as severely. She encouraged us, "Don't let your past halt you when considering Christ. There's no sin too grave, no condition unforgivable. You'll have a new life." Quite true, but what I struggled with was the golden picture that followed her acceptance of Christ. I leaned over to my companion and scribbled on the back of my program, *What about when your past is your present?*

While it's true that you become a new creation in Christ (see 2 Corinthians 5:17), I caution you against relaxing into an expectation of invincibility, or to the other extreme, judging yourself too harshly for your continued struggles with temptation. You are not alone; others have gone and are going through the same thing, and Jesus Himself suffered completely under every temptation known to man, yet without falling to sin. He made you. He knows you. He even knows why you fall, and He lives in mercy to change and heal you.

First John 3:9 says, "No one who is born of God will continue to sin, because God's seed remains in him; he cannot go on sinning, because he has been born of God." It's true. The Holy Spirit living in you will not allow you to remain unchanged. But don't hang the armor in the closet just yet. Remember that vulnerability remains and therefore so must a blazing vigilance in Christ. Don't ever consider the sins you've conquered in the past now suddenly powerless to tempt you; nor should you consider yourself impervious to the sins of which you think yourself incapable. If you leave a certain gate unguarded because you're sure the enemy won't be coming from that direction, the enemy will eventually learn that particular gate is the best way in.

Vulnerability remains and therefore so must a blazing vigilance in Christ.

God often walks devotedly by our sides even through the temptations we refuse to avoid, knowing the decisions we'll make in His favor further down the road. Then when we've dug into our blindness too deeply or for too long, He stoops, spits in the mud and wipes our eyes clear (see John 9:6-7). He gives us yet another chance to make the right choice. He calls again, patient and familiar, *Who do you love, child? Come and walk with Me.*

Don't be afraid of your failures. Fear God, but allow Him to fashion your failures into tools. Watch what God can do with dirt. Choose always to unashamedly deliver to Him your handful of dirt and ask Him to work His wonders.

Grace is not just for your yesterdays, your forgivable past. Grace is for today. Grace will be for tomorrow. His mercies are new every morning (see Lamentations 3:23). Wrap them around you, and get back to work. The battle is not a simple one; it is raging without rest. But it is finished in Christ. Remain in Him.

Reflections

1. Is there something you consider the largest mistake in your life, a moment when you fell the hardest? How did God use that time or that event to draw you closer to Him? What did God teach you through the valley of that experience?

2. If there was nothing that came from that incident or era—somehow strengthening, changing or teaching you or others—have you asked God to use it now for good, to teach you now whatever you were supposed to learn?

3. Did you ever have an opportunity to use what you learned from that situation to help someone else who was facing the same trauma or temptation? How did you help that person?

Prayer

Lord Jesus, help me to remember but one thing: I need You. Father, this battle will never be over as long as I'm still on this earth. Let me rage against it, with You before me at all times. Let me not be deceived in the slightest, by myself, by others or by the grave and destructive schemes of Satan. Be my eyes, Lord, and don't ever let me walk on ahead of You. Don't let go of me and don't let me let go of You. Knock it down, Lord, whatever would rip my hand from Yours. Ignite an unquenchable fire that rises against that which would singe my soul. Make me bold and yet so aware that I have no strength that is not completely Yours. How many ways can I cry, Father, "lead [me] not into temptation, but deliver [me] from evil" (Matthew 6:13, KJV)? Let it always be my cry. Let me never leave Your side. I am Yours and Yours alone. Let me stay that way. Amen.

25

A Divine Purpose

*From one man he made every nation of men, that they should in-
habit the whole earth; and he determined the times set for them
and the exact places where they should live. God did this so that
men would seek him and perhaps reach out for him and find him,
though he is not far from each one of us. (Acts 17:26-27)*

You could have a divine purpose. I don't mean could as in
"might," but could as in "can," as in it's there for the taking, guaranteed. You need only choose to take it.

My hometown pastor, David George, is someone I greatly ad-
mire for his gifted grasp of the balance between humility—the
reality of the human estate, where there is nothing we can offer
God worth more than "filthy rags" (Isaiah 64:6)—and wisdom,
which is the reality of our intended beauty in the sum of Christ.
He recognizes who we are versus who God is and our utter inability versus His perfect ability, that we are simultaneously imperfect yet eternally perfected in Him. He said in a recent
sermon, "Only when you realize your lack of beauty will you discover the beauty He's realized for you—the beauty of yourself as
you were meant to be, the beauty of a love perfectly matched, the
beauty of His creation meant to be His glory. When you realize
what you are not is when you will discover the greatest measure
of what you were meant to be."

Hebrews 10:14 says, "By one sacrifice he has made perfect forever those who are being made holy." You are in the middle of this process, but as far as the end of the story goes, as far as what He sees in you right now, you have already been made perfect. "It is finished" (John 19:30).

Just a few weeks ago, this concept hit me like a lightning bolt in yet another new way, one that finally elucidated the point for me from His point of view. I'd attended an artists' Bible study here in my hometown of Sacramento where we were reading a book on creativity that mentioned God's call to "all who are skilled" to craft the ark of the covenant according to His design. He even called the artists by name.

> Then Moses said to the Israelites, "See, the LORD has chosen Bezalel son of Uri, the son of Hur, of the tribe of Judah, and he has filled him with the Spirit of God, with skill, ability and knowledge in all kinds of crafts—to make artistic designs for work in gold, silver and bronze, to cut and set stones, to work in wood and to engage in all kinds of artistic craftsmanship. And he has given both him and Oholiab son of Ahisamach, of the tribe of Dan, the ability to teach others. He has filled them with skill to do all kinds of work as craftsmen, designers, embroiderers in blue, purple and scarlet yarn and fine linen, and weavers—all of them master craftsmen and designers. (Exodus 35:30-35)

As I was reading those words, the picture of God's desire became clear. The work of the hands of the artists, whose talents He had gifted in the first place, was the *place* He chose to house His Spirit. The product of their talents *was,* by His call, the Holy of Holies. Their *use* of their talents is where God sat.

Some he made woodworkers and some he made metalworkers. Some he's made mothers and some soldiers, some presidents and some preachers. But the gift of our talents, given by His hand, perfected by His name, is where He still houses His glory, where He chooses to rest His Spirit within our presence while we wander this desert toward the Promised Land. Like the pinnacle of the literal, original ark, our use of the gifts He's given us is His temporal sanctuary while we travel toward the permanent.

Don't let your own perception of unworthiness stop you. Grasping that unworthiness is actually a victory. Some people never get to a point of accepting that there is a need for God in their hearts, for both love and forgiveness. It's an accomplishment to get to the point where you appreciate your own insufficiency as part of the story. So trust Him with your faults and failings. Trust His promises of forgiveness and restoration. Grab on to His offer of redemption and be prepared for a process, a long road, a commitment and a covenant where only one of you will fall short—repeatedly. But He knew that before He "signed the papers" on the cross, before He gave you life. Whatever His purposes in you, He's been laying them down long before you were born. He might only bring those purposes to fruition after you leave this life, but you can assume unimaginable intent and perfection where His precision is involved.

It's impossible to imagine how He might multiply the improbable into a miracle of the ages.

Take for example the story of Corrie ten Boom, one of the gentlest yet loudest voices of the gospel in this past century. In 1844, according to his journals, Willem ten Boom, Corrie's grandfather, was "moved of God" to begin praying for the nation of Israel. This was not during an era in which the nation of Israel was necessarily a primary social focus, so it was an uncommon calling. But there in Haarlem, Denmark, in a little house called the Beje, Willem gathered his pastor and neighbors into his home on a regular basis to pray for God's chosen people. As it followed, Willem's son Casper grew, moved out, returned to the house after his father's passing and raised his children back at home in the original Beje. Then in 1944, *exactly* 100 years later, that same room where Willem had prayed became "The Hiding Place." Corrie was fifty-five years old before her highest calling began to take shape, a calling whose foundations had been laid in prayer a hundred years prior. It's neither too late in your life nor too early in the course of events to begin. Put your life in God's hands and ask for the purpose only He could weave.

You have a purpose that heaven finds imperative, crucial enough to engage the hands of God.

Another Christian whose higher calling came late but strong was President Ronald Wilson Reagan. On his fiftieth birthday, Reagan was standing in the middle of his life as a Democratic actor, discharged from the military, with a mild interest in politics. It wasn't until *twenty-six* years later that he stood, as the Republican fortieth president of the United States of America, at the Brandenburg Gate and shouted through the unfolding reaches of history, "Mr. Gorbachev, tear down this wall!"

Are these callings too large and unimaginable to apply to you? Consider this: A wonderful Jamaican woman from my church in New York dropped this bit of profundity in front of our entire congregation when we were all searching the Scriptures for a "larger" truth. Her name was Joyce Brown, and she was one of several hundred women who had gathered at Calvary Baptist on a Saturday to enjoy an afternoon with Anne Graham Lotz (whom I highly regard). During an open forum, we were discussing as a group the lessons within the loaves and fishes miracle (Matthew 14:13-21; Mark 6:30-44; Luke 9:10-17; John 6:1-15), raising our hands and "imparting our wisdom," when Mrs. Brown stood up and very simply stated in prime Jamaican accent, "What I would like to know is who is da mama who was sitteen at home packing da sack lunch for her little boy?" Brilliant. Even if you are "sitteen" at home packing sack lunches and folding laundry, do it as unto the Lord (see 1 Corinthians 10:31). It's impossible to imagine how He might multiply the improbable, the utterly mundane, into a miracle of the ages.

To repeat what I said earlier: You could have a divine purpose. You may not provide an underground escape route for thousands of Jewish refugees; you may not become an American president. But you do have a purpose that heaven finds imperative and crucial enough to engage the hands of God. I don't care who you are, where you are, what has or has not happened in your life. If you are here, breathe deeply the breath of life that He's bestowed and realize that it comes straight from His hand, with intention for you. You are seen, you are called, you are chosen. He doesn't need us to run this universe of His, but He's elected to build it with relationship and love for us. Not a detail is lost or unable to be used for good.

You. You are on His mind and a part of His plan. You are His inspiration. He has an idea; sit down with Him and listen. There's no imagining what He might begin or finish in you. I said above, "You may not provide an underground escape route; you may not become a president," but in reality, you just might. Tomorrow can happen so quickly, and His ability to move His plan is unlimited. His plan could be anything. It may be just a call to prayer that spiritually prepares a famous Hiding Place. It may be a turning point of history. It may be a word to a child that changes the course of his life. It might be as simple as packing a sack lunch. Whatever it is, are you listening? Are you ready? Are you willing?

Reflections

1. Do you believe God could do something through your life that would have a tremendous spiritual and historical impact?
2. Do you believe that God could use you to entirely alter the course of someone's life—or many lives? Are you prepared to ask for those opportunities?
3. Are you watching for what He might be doing for others through your life? Are you listening for the small directions of the Holy Spirit, trusting that they might have a greater purpose than you could ever imagine, a purpose that you might even see in your lifetime?

Prayer

Lord God, I forget to believe, sometimes, in the size of what You're willing—and prepared—to do, what You're trying to do through and for Your people, what You're longing to do both for Your glory and for our restoration. I forget that You used a single man to walk an entire nation of Your people into Your promised land. I forget that the unfathomable miracles in Your Word were often built on the willingness—even hesitant willingness—of a single serving soul, most often every bit as small, frightened or underqualified as I consider myself to be. Help me to adopt an unusual preparedness, looking for a larger plan than I would dream of. Change Your world in Your way and use me. I am just as small and afraid as the rest of them, but I am willing. Whatever it is, almighty God, here I am. Use me. Amen.

26

The Other Love Story

Do not turn aside from any of the commands I give you today, to the right or to the left, following other gods and serving them. (Deuteronomy 28:14)

Love the Lord your God with all your heart and with all your soul and with all your mind and with all your strength. (Mark 12:30)

Have you ever been in love?

Before we get into the deeper covenant of love or discuss the qualities of "agape," let's just start with that initial explosion of curiosity and chemistry. Let's talk about the way you feel about that person to whom you are uncontrollably drawn, whom you can't get out of your mind for a second, who turns you into a child with his or her make-or-break-your-day influence on your emotions. I believe the great logician Thumper (the bunny from *Bambi*) referred to it as being "twitterpated."

It can be a cliché reference—and belittling if taken too far—to make a valentine out of Jesus. But from the Psalms to contemporary compositions like *The Sacred Romance* by Brent Curtis and John Eldredge we find it both an obvious and an accurate exercise to explore divine love through comparisons to the lesser human paradigms. Usually the comparison is in taking the beauty of the love we have for one another and multiplying or perfecting it to get just a glimpse of His heart for us. But recently a different angle caught my attention—the power of the heart to pull you off God's path—bringing fresh light to how fervently I seek the Lord (or don't) compared to how often I allow Him to be overshadowed by earthly idols and counterparts.

Before we go any further, I want to make sure we're all on the same page (literally), and that we don't skip over the fundamental point of the last paragraph: that our gifts of love on this earth *are* modeled after the love of God and given to us by His hand to share with one another. God Himself constantly heralds the magnitudes of love, calling love for Him and for each other, respectively, the two greatest commandments (Matthew 22:34-40). He celebrates love in verses like "the greatest of these is love" (1 Corinthians 13:13), in the gift of marriage, in the definition of creation and the gospel— all of these being the very substance of love. There is no greater force than love, which equals everything from kindness to salvation. God *is* love, and He's given that gift to us. But this particular devotional—while not intending at all to diminish the splendor of supernatural and human love and how the two were created to intertwine—is an entirely separate discussion of "other" loves: the decoys, the diversions of idols and temptations, the things for which we sometimes take our attentions away from God and honor *instead of* Him.

In God's immaculate way of using "all things for good" (see Romans 8:28), He stepped in during a season when I'd become distracted by a far-too-accredited idol. I was beginning to feel affected by someone I already knew God didn't want in my life—even found myself struggling against God—but He faithfully used my misdirected focus to teach me how to seek Him better. It was an effective illustration of a fresh way of thinking—a fresh way I thought I already knew. It stirred up a million questions: Where is my inspired attention? How much do I explore the one true language of love compared to its counterfeit? How feverishly does my heart seek after the right presence in my life?

It was halfway through my third reading of a love letter, as I started to feel my heart slipping from God's strength to my frailty, that the spiritual caveat sounded: Why do we give more weight to the love of human beings, in their messages and confessions of love, than to an eternal, unwavering God and every word of His messages, His confessions of love? Why do we believe unproven, emotional, human-sized promises more readily than the unbreakable, passionate Word of God? We even cry harder over struggles with false, weightless loves, which are conditional and temporal, than over the sin that comes between us and the unconditional, perfect love of Christ. Why do we sometimes run *from* Him and run *to* what hurts us?

Why do we believe human-sized promises more readily than the unbreakable Word of God?

"Why" is hard to answer, beyond the simple fact that it's a spiritual manipulation. Satan is forever trying to convince us of anything that is a lie. A pastor of mine once said, "Prayer is so difficult *because* it is so powerful." We can say the same for anything that carries us in a God-ward direction. The smallest choice in favor of God is more significant than we would give it—or ourselves—credit for. Likewise, the smallest decisions which walk us away from Him are just as equipped to multiply, although they are not equal on the scale, because a Victor has written the final chapter. He'll let us make our own choices, but He will not let us die beneath them. He'll allow us to become broken, but only in ways the Shepherd's hands can easily repair.

So while "why" is left undeclared, the remedy is in zealously pursuing the opposite. Pursue the other love story (God's) until you understand it, until it grips your heart as easily as any idolistic love affair and then surpasses it into more than you've imagined, more than your mind has ever conceived (see 1 Corinthians 2:9).

Do it literally, in the limited way your human spirit would tend to, and let God build it into His idea of love. Begin with the "language of love" mentioned earlier. Have you ever read and reread a love letter? And reread and reread? Now ask yourself if you've ever read God's Word in the same manner of intensity, hope and discovery, poring over the arrangement of words and dwelling on the character of their writer. I asked myself, *Have I ever really searched, weighed and cherished God's Word and the "man" behind them as fervently as I'm searching this fleeting human love letter now?*

His love comes off the page and becomes so much more alive than it was before.

I'm less talented than your average Christian at grasping the literal love of God. Believing it is one thing; understanding it is quite another. I know me, and I cannot fathom how Someone who knows me better than I know myself, who knows my heart, good and bad, and who is Himself the only existing righteousness, could call me His beloved. But I began reading His Word with the same questions I'd been wasting on the far less worthy words of man.

What is His nature and the tone of His heart when He speaks certain phrases? What is His intention when He repeats favored truths from Genesis to Revelation again and again throughout my day? What secrets can I learn about the heart behind the words, and what more revealing things might He be saying if I deeply consider

the elements of what He's written? When I seek the personality behind the message, the love slowly takes form. The Holy Spirit responds, as promised, to a hunger for His love, and He begins to
sculpt the image within my heart, before my eyes. His love comes
off the page and becomes more than acceptable; it becomes understandable and so much more alive than it was before.

He stood me on my feet and, suddenly, instead of focusing my
attentions toward any other interest, it's God's image I'm seeking in the crowd, His whereabouts that are my primary curiosity,
even His adoration that moves me most.

For the first time in my life, I fell in love with God, after loving
Him for a lifetime and yet being completely confused or frustrated by anyone's references to "falling in love with God." I had
been especially frustrated by all the singles' books suggesting fulfillment with Christ as my "spouse." I understood what they
meant and believed I embraced my own version of that, my
equivalent. After all, I'd followed Him passionately to the ends of
the earth—or to New York City, which is pretty much the same
thing. I'd sacrificed what I couldn't imagine; I'd leapt in faith
further than I'd ever thought possible. I trusted Him with my
heart. But suddenly, now, I fell for Him. I had a very new appreciation—a finished security, the sensation of being in love—yet
in addition I had the perfection of knowing it was with God, who
is both the source and the recipient of that love.

I still have a hard time with that phrasing, "falling in love with
God." It seems irreverent when referring to the God of Abraham,
Isaac and Jacob. But I got over that when I realized the radical ex-
pressions of love He's already used in regard to me (to each of us) in
His Word—not to mention His actions that follow those words.

Love has drawn people through the ages to do large things.
It's a compelling force that drives us to great lengths, both positive and negative, destructive and redemptive. Look at what
love compelled God to do for us. How might we be able to live

if we would allow ourselves to be just as strongly compelled by the always-healing influence of love for God?

More strongly than you have ever pursued the acceptance of man, more stirred than you have ever been by passing promises and ephemeral affections of man, pursue the love of God. Let the eternal become a love letter alive within you—changing, perfecting, satisfying. It is love accomplished. Let it in.

Reflections

1. Do you ever find yourself clinging more desperately to human promises of love and caring than to the promises of God?

2. Have you ever pored over the Scriptures with as much eagerness as you might give to a letter from a loved one or cherished the intentions of love in certain words, all while considering and savoring the personality behind them, the heart that put the message into place?

Prayer

Father, forgive me for at times seeking the love of others more fervently than I seek You, for reveling in the winning of it with more delight than I take in the already-given gift of Your waiting love. Help me to understand Your perfect passion and to seek it as my heart's greatest gladness. Help me still to appreciate fully the love and companionship You created between human beings, but remind me that human love is a mere shadow of what can be found resting in Your presence, laughing with Your joy, sharing Your mercy and Your desires, simply knowing You. Let me realize this love between us. As You fill my life still with others to love, to serve and to cherish, my Lord God, be the only One I need. Amen.

27

Trust His Higher Sight

Trust in the LORD with all your heart
and lean not on your own understanding;
in all your ways acknowledge him,
and he will make your paths straight. (Proverbs 3:5-6)

It's another gorgeous day in northern California with only slight clouds, which the sun separates easily to drench what's below. But just a moment ago, thunder ripped through the sky with no warning, for no understandable reason. It hasn't been raining today, nor is it expected to, and this isn't the East Coast where sunny rainstorms often unexpectedly burst through the clouds. Nonetheless, the thunder was undeniably there. There is no reason to believe it, looking around me now, but I trust what I heard. I'm familiar with how my ears work, and pretty sure of them; therefore, there must have been thunder.

How much more sure can we be of God's presence and His promises that His ways are perfect and unchanging? We will spend an entire lifetime learning how to trust Him not by our human standards of trust, but to the levels that His sovereignty merits, and we will never, in this lifetime, achieve the full volume of it.

There's a true story from just north of my hometown which perfectly illustrates why we must learn to trust God's sovereignty as a sure thing, despite what we may be able to see. It begins with a woman alone in her car, being tailed by a truck driver in an eighteen-wheeler on the narrow highways of the Sierra foothills. Throughout the region there had been a rash of instances with tailgating tractor trailers that had ended gruesomely, and this woman was fearful her fate would be the same. The semi was nearly on her bumper, matching her speed, risking the steep inclines and sharp curves to keep up the chase. She swerved off the road at the first available exit and stopped in the middle of a truck-stop parking lot. Door open, motor running, she ran toward the diner. Tears blanketing her face, she called for help and watched through the window as the truck driver, who had continued to tail her all the way into the parking lot, jumped out of his cab, ran to her car, flung open the rear door and pulled out a man who had been hiding in her backseat. From his higher vantage point, perched high atop his rig, the truck driver had spotted the real danger and stayed in close pursuit in order to protect, not to harm.

The Lord calls, *Walk with Me and trust My eyes, My wisdom. Trust My love for you.* How we feel about Him or our circumstances, or how we react and act toward Him, doesn't deter His concern for our real danger. May we learn when we see the lights in our rearview mirror not to be afraid, not to fight or twist away, not to complain about a relentless or strict God on our tails, but to knowingly pull over alongside that day's road and trust a Higher Sight to deliver us into His plan.

The trucker story always reminds me of a story Dr. James Dobson tells in one of his sermons about watching a gerbil in a cage working day and night at his "escape techniques," climbing and nudging at the screen. Meanwhile, Dr. Dobson could both see and understand what the gerbil could not: the cat in the corner, watching, wishing the gerbil would succeed. The gerbil, if he prayed like a man, would be whining to God about why He won't answer his prayers and let him succeed at his efforts.

Even when we steadfastly believe God's promises, trust can still be such a hard thing to do without being able to see the big picture for ourselves. But God didn't condemn us to living our lives as frustrated gerbils. He explains—both in His Word and through His Spirit, our daily counselor—how different things look from His vantage point. Sometimes He lifts us onto His shoulders to show us the view; sometimes He leaves us safely at His feet and says, "Just trust Me." Trust, like faith, is not an emotion, but a decision, a determination. Most of the time the decision contrasts with our immediate emotions. But trust, *especially* when it's difficult, is part of God's formula. When we tie our own blindfolds willingly and take hold of the Father's hand, we are handing Him an irresistible lump of clay. He is the Potter. He is a Master Sculptor. He has built nations with a lump of trust, a leap of faith.

When we tie our own blindfolds willingly and take hold of the Father's hand, we are handing Him an irresistible lump of clay.

Practice trusting Him. It not only gets easier; it becomes enticing. Suddenly, when you see the Egyptians bearing down from the top of the hill, dust and stones flying from beneath the chariot wheels, you find such a ready trust that you're instinctively prepared to turn and wait. With a glint in your eye and a trusting spirit that knows the power and the character of the God you serve, you wait with animated anticipation for the very sea to open up before you.

It's a *chance*. This could be the moment of miracle, even if the entire miracle is merely your ability to discover an unwavering trust, just as against hope, Abraham believed (see Romans 4:18).

What a privilege to expect such things in the course of a day, in the face of opposition. If He knows the changing number of hairs on our heads (see Luke 12:7), knows our prayers before they're spoken (see Isaiah 65:24), knows us and our purposes before we're even conceived (see Jeremiah 1:5), then He certainly knows where we're standing now and what might be coming down the hill. I tried to promise to God one time, "You know my heart, Lord. You can depend on me." The answer to that prayer was, *You're right. I know your heart and you do not. Trust Me, not yourself, and least of all your heart. Trust my Word, trust Me.* Trust Him to gauge your heart better than you can, for "the heart is deceitful above all things" (Jeremiah 17:9).

He has built nations with a lump of trust, a leap of faith.

One of my favorite illustrations describes a man trapped in a raging stream, holding on to a precarious limb, barely keeping his head above the current. He gasps for air, while his grip becomes weaker and his heart more dismayed. But just around the corner, so close, the river empties into calm waters. He would be safe if he would just let go and let the waters carry him.

Granted, it might be hard to take a chance at trusting the river to take you to the sea. But there's no such thing as chance with the God of Abraham. Let His waters carry you. He sees into the backseat, across the carpet to the cat, around the corner of the river. He sees you.

When you decide to trust Him, He moves. And as He moves He will use you—to heal, to praise, to become a psalm that tells the world what can be done when you follow a pillar of fire and a pillar of cloud into a wild desert. It's an odd way to embark on a search for freedom, but it's hard to resist when, in Jesus, you've gotten a taste of the Promised Land.

The sacrifice of trust can be gut-wrenching at times. I often wonder if Moses' hair turned white from seeing God or from stress. But start with a step onto just one rung of His promises. It makes God dance. It makes Him want to tuck you safely in the cleft and pass all His glory before you (see Exodus 33:22). Pick up your tent. Be curious of Him. Be sure of Him. And go.

Reflections

1. Was there ever a situation in your life that turned out much differently than you thought it was going to? Can you look back and understand what God was doing or trying to tell you beforehand?
2. What is your first response to a problem or a threat? Are you truly able to look at a troubling situation and say, "Thank You, Lord"? Can you trust what He sees from His higher vantage point and hand Him your steadfast faith?
3. When you have to take a leap of faith, ask Him to give you a greater confidence or conviction in His character, the same yesterday, today and tomorrow.

Prayer

Lord, I know Your ways are not like mine. Your sight is unfathomably higher, Your knowledge inconceivably more vast. So I am willing to leap and let You catch me and carry me. When I am trying to get to a goal I can see and You begin walking me in the opposite direction, help me to trust You in the way You're leading me. It can be confusing, Lord, based on what I can see from here, but I know that my faith is "not by sight." Nor is any of this "by might" or "by power," but all of it by Your Spirit alone (see Zechariah 4:6). So I'm ready to trust You (make me ready). I want to live by trust. I want to go where You are going. I want the kind of faith that makes me able to pick up my tent and move my family at a single, clear word from You. I want to be Yours to that degree. I'm sure this will take guts, practice and perhaps cold feet now and then. But mold me, Lord. Wrench me if You must into a trusting servant, because I know Your ways are higher, and Your way is the way I want. Amen.

28

Cosmic Perfection

*In him we were also chosen, having been predestined according to
the plan of him who works out everything in conformity with the
purpose of his will, in order that we, who were the first to hope in
Christ, might be for the praise of his glory. (Ephesians 1:11-12)*

Have you ever considered that complete cosmic perfection is, in Christ, attainable? Not just at the peaks, but in the valleys—even in struggle or brokenness, weakness or loss, in any life, under any circumstance. It's not always what we picture or shoot for as perfection. But if it is a puzzle piece whose shapes have been carved out by creation's most talented carpenter, it will fit tightly into the intended, perfect picture.

I do find it funny that "cosmic perfection" is only one "s" short of "*comic* perfection." The comedy isn't missed in comparing our vision of perfection with God's. But even in our limited understanding—knowing we don't understand most of the time—we can intrinsically learn the nature of God's Word and believe it, believe that whatever issue "it" is in our lives, it is only imperfect when manipulated into our idea of right. Yet when left in His hands it is perfected. We are perfected in His hands.

I remember when I first began to transition from a life I *thought* was God's into a life that was *truly* lived for Him. It was all very fresh, so the difference between the two lives was even more noticeable. I loved the new taste of verses like, "Delight yourself in the LORD and he will give you the desires of your heart" (Psalm 37:4). For years that verse had been a thorn to me, and now it became such a pleasure as I realized that when I begin to genuinely delight in the Lord, when He is the only real need on my list, my wish list begins to change—dramatically. He *can* give me all the desires of my heart, because the more I delight in Him, the more I only want what He wants. I can see more concretely the reality of what will build me and what will harm me.

> *This confidence in His movement is something we'd be smart to master.*

I'm at a point in life where nothing is secure on the human level. Everything is in transition. I'm not even in my own home right now. Yet I've never felt more "settled." It's a solid and satisfied feeling, a place I'd prefer to live all the time, and I'm beginning to see how possible that is. Though this strength comes and goes in life, drugged by the "human condition," I've finally begun to sense something: Yes, it is true that we will not be perfected until we are before Him and rid of our sinful tendencies, but there *is* a place of constant perfection of circumstances.

This confidence in His movement is something we'd be smart to master. Through uncertain circumstances, personal or global, there really is one solid road to stand on. We talk about the peaks and valleys, the struggles and the mountaintop experiences, but is it possible to fly a straight line through all of them? If we're relying on the same armor, the same God, the same promises, then why wouldn't it be possible? The heart's cry may change as rapidly as the Psalms, from weeping to joy and back again (see Psalm

30:5), but the voice behind the Psalms was a man always after God's own heart—and still further, behind David's voice was the ever steady voice of an unchanging God.

When we find Him entirely, He is the sufficiency of any single beat of our hearts, and He will hold us there, perfectly, in the center of His will. We will be a complement to whatever and whomever we encounter. We will have the joy of being, for the sake of those around us, someone who has discovered the secret of resting in a foot-in-footprint perfect trust of God's path. I reiterate: It's a wavering battle, but stability within it is obtainable. It takes practice; it takes trust; it takes knowing it's possible in the first place.

Step one is simply seeking trust, wanting that portion of the relationship, wanting to be able to trust more than wanting all the answers. Step two is learning to trust for trust's sake, because He is trustworthy and as a product of faith. Step three (which is really about a million steps beyond step two, so it may take time) is fully adopting the "everything is perfect if it's in His hands" rule—understanding it, believing it and living by it.

We graduate to a higher level when we leap from asking Him to help us trust Him to believing in His utter sovereignty and that, for no reason I'll ever understand, His sovereignty is intent on our best interests. There's a fascinating dualism between "What is man that you are mindful of him?" (Psalm 8:4) and "In all things God works for the good of those who love him" (Romans 8:28). Look at just a few of the Scriptures that call for us to understand His perfection:

> He is the Rock, his works are perfect,
>   and all his ways are just.
> A faithful God who does no wrong,
>   upright and just is he. (Deuteronomy 32:4)

> As for God, his way is perfect;
>   the word of the LORD is flawless.

He is a shield
    for all who take refuge in him. (2 Samuel 22:31)

It is God who arms me with strength
    and makes my way perfect.
(2 Samuel 22:33; Psalm 18:32)

One perfect in knowledge is with you. (Job 36:4)

But when perfection comes, the imperfect disappears.
(1 Corinthians 13:10)

Let us fix our eyes on Jesus, the author and perfecter of our faith, who for the joy set before him endured the cross, scorning its shame, and sat down at the right hand of the throne of God. Consider him who endured such opposition from sinful men, so that you will not grow weary and lose heart. (Hebrews 12:2-3)

More than asking for open eyes to see the path, ask Him also to make you entirely comfortable with your eyes closed, as we discussed earlier—be *that* sure of His sovereignty. If the path is still cloaked in impenetrable darkness, reach out and ask for His hand. When you feel it tightly wrapped around yours, don't worry about where the path leads; just trust Him. He will not let go; He will not lead you into despair. He will lead you into a style of living that, if you learn to speak His language, begins to look like unwavering perfection.

Lest you think I'm talking about God as a genie, be mindful of the fact that this level of trust takes a *lot* of trust—trust of His Word, His character and all you have not seen—because it is exactly this level of trust that brings you, sometimes, into the most trying applications of it. He knows who will trust Him through the hardest tasks, who will, even if they struggle, ultimately not let go when tempted to deny Him or curse Him. Sometimes living in His perfect will brings on what might seem to be, by earthly standards, an absolute *im*perfection.

One of the most tender things I've ever read is Dale Evans Rogers' *Angel Unaware*. She takes on the handicap and eventual death of her young child not as a slight from God or a mistake or an imperfection. As she shares this experience she senses the perfection in what we, as humans, call an imperfect story. Though we're human and bound to grieve, to cry, to wish the story could have been different, even in the midst of tears, anger and emotion, we can rest in the unattached knowledge that our struggle is perfect in His knowledge of all things considered. Whatever it is, there is a reason for it, reason enough for Him to ask us to endure the hurt and trust Him.

When we find Him entirely, He is the sufficiency of any single beat of our hearts.

This is, again, like Calvary (it seems every element we've discussed can be taken back to and compared to Calvary). There was a reason large enough to necessitate the hurt of Christ's, and of God's, own heart. He endured it for what it brought and for what it meant. He endured the literal, physical human pain of the cross, the spiritual rending of Christ's heart as He bore the weight of every sin and separation from His Father, the cosmic sorrow as God forced Himself, for reason of all mankind, to turn His head and allow His Son to bear the unearned. He accepted the loss, the knowledge, perhaps the "temptation," for lack of a better word, to stop it all. Christ could have called "legions of angels" (Matthew 26:53-54). But realize that Calvary was not an unavoidable given. It was a choice. He chose to drink the fuller cup. Though it looked at the time like the darkest, most unreserved moment of imperfection, it was the brightest, most absolute, accomplished perfection. Between the two, trusting what the Father designed, Jesus chose a terrible, painful, wonderful, eternal perfection. Thank God, quite literally.

No matter where you are, consider the absolute perfection of the day, the biggest picture, the end of the story. Believe its perfection as He uses even what we've broken for good. Take Him at His word.

Reflections

1. Is there something troubling you in life for which you can't imagine there being a purpose? Are you ready to hand it to the Lord, believing that if it's in your life there's a reason for it?
2. How closely are you watching for what the purpose may be? And once you discover the purpose unfolding, are you ready to respond accordingly? Are you ready to serve God within that purpose and to be grateful for what God was doing all along?

Prayer

Lord, even when I have learned to trust You, learned that You use all things for good, it's still so far out of reach for me to imagine that even the horrific things that I sometimes face can be considered a part of perfection. But I acknowledge that I am not You and I cannot see as You can. I acknowledge that somehow the horror and darkness of Calvary was the greatest perfection ever achieved. I am grateful that I serve a God who understands sacrifice, loss and pain, and who is the author of the formula that turns that pain into something as bright and perfect as Christ. Let me trust You to be the author of that same height of perfection in my life, to turn every loss, every sacrifice, every darkness into a greater light than I could have known was possible. I hand You my life and invite You to be the "perfecter of [my] faith" (Hebrews 12:2). Take it, Lord, and turn it all into a perfect light. Amen.

29

A Very Simple Gospel

And this gospel of the kingdom will be preached in the whole world as a testimony to all nations. (Matthew 24:14)

The image of Christ in the manger is chock full of symbolism, and we use it, lean on it, all the time. We make replicas of the manger for crèches—Popsicle sticks and yarn glued together in Sunday school, live nativities with someone's volunteered newborn, mangers of all shapes and symbolic sizes. I even have an awful white, glittery manger-and-stable candle I'm admittedly saving for Christmas—one of the few measly Christmas decorations I own as a single woman. The symbolism of the manger speaks to us—mostly at Christmas, but always powerfully—of a simple, finished gospel.

How? As my dear friend Dr. Gaddy recently pointed out, Jesus, the Bread of Life, was born in a *feeding* trough. Beyond the imagery of humility, glory in unsought places and the unusual character of God, the manger demonstrates that Christ came as the final satisfaction of the need of humankind, that we might eat and be filled, drink and never thirst (see John 6:35). At the Last Supper, He broke the bread as a symbol of His soon-to-be brokenness and gave it to His disciples to eat, saying, "Do this in remembrance of me" (Luke

22:19); "eat of my flesh, drink of my blood" (see 1 Corinthians 11:23-25); "I am the living bread that came down from heaven. If anyone eats of this bread, he will live forever. This bread is my flesh, which I will give for the life of the world" (John 6:51). It was the selfsame gospel offered in His last moments as in His first breath, when God, who wastes no image, laid His Son in a manger, the Bread of Life given "for the life of the world."

We could stand to visit that symbolism year round. It's perfect. In an average Christian life, while exploring "truths and applications" in Bible studies and small groups galore, how often do we stop to consider the simplicity, finality and sufficiency of the gospel itself? Do we ever dwell on it, espousingly, appreciatively, comprehensively? When telling others about Him, do we try to slug through the revelation of the entire Bible, Genesis to Revelation, arguing issues and denominations, having forgotten to lay down a very simple gospel?

The symbolism of the manger speaks to us of a simple, finished gospel.

It's one of the things that made Billy Graham, Billy Graham— a man who has not only reached billions through multiplication, but who has reached the *world* beyond the Church. Who else has been able to popularize the things of Jesus within the "must-see-TV" lineup—and not just through "shows with redemptive values" but with the unadulterated, message-of-salvation, just-as-I-am gospel?

Graham's broad reach is not because of his celebrity, as some would argue, because there was a day when he wasn't famous, and he carried the same message then into the out-of-bounds. How did he become so effective then? By stating the simple gospel of the

Lord Jesus Christ—crucified, risen and coming again—then standing back and letting Jesus be Lord. He embodied the gospel and added nothing, especially not apology for the Word of God. He delivered truth in love, utter assuredness and utter acceptance. I remind you, Billy Graham is not the "the man with the secret." He spoke what Jesus gave to all mankind. It's the same gospel we all have, and it has the same power of the same Spirit behind it.

Be bold with the Word, and sure of it, both with yourself and with others. Visit the depth of the straight gospel: "For God so loved the world that he gave his one and only Son, that whoever believes in him shall not perish but have eternal life" (John 3:16). Dwell on that alone.

It's easy to keep coming back to Christmas-related references because there is no other time throughout the year when we're so "allowed" to publicly acknowledge Christ, or when we take the liberty to. It's amazing what the world becomes when people start to speak of His birth and sing of His truths around the world. Even if it's half-hearted in places, or partnered with Santa in others, the words are still being spoken, and "It" happens. They call it "the spirit of Christmas," and it is, if you capitalize *Spirit*.

For me, there's even the excitement of discovering Christ anew in some way as I watch Him come to life in the world around me at Christmastime. Every twentieth or thirtieth time through a certain hymn, a phrase will leap out at me as a truth I've never considered literally before. It was at the Christmas Eve candlelight service at my home church several years ago when I was struck by all the lyrics to "What Child Is This?" The title itself is the entire point of the gospel: "Who do you say I am?" (Matthew 16:15; Mark 8:29; Luke 9:20).

So many times in His life, Jesus followed "Himself" with that question. When people faced a reflection of faith or asked for a miracle, Jesus asked, "Do you believe that I can do this?" (see Matthew 9:28). Essentially he was asking, "Do you believe I am the Messiah?" because who else could do such things? When Jesus multiplied the loaves and fishes and knit the gospel elements into the provision as we discussed previously, He immediately followed that interwoven presentation of the gospel by posing the question to Peter, "Who do you say that I am?" It's a question asked by His mere existence. How does your spirit respond? Who do you say that He is? Like Peter, my spirit cries with *its* mere existence, "I say you are the Son of God" (see Matthew 16:16; Mark 8:29; Luke 9:20).

"God so loved the world" . . . Dwell on that alone.

But we're not even to my favorite line in the song yet. The third verse ends with the line, "Good Christian fear, for sinners here, the silent Word is pleading." There, it's captured: His mere existence already pleading *by* His existence. The Jasper Stone of Heaven, the Son of God took on the humanity of flesh, and by the living palm of an infant hand, destined to feel the mercy-wood of the cross, was ready to plead on our behalf. God heard from His throne the Son who had just been at His side, "pleading for sinners here." Consider this gospel.

In that initial moment of the first Noël, "God so loved the world" (John 3:16)—and ever before and after. Merry Christmas from Jesus to man. "Me? I say you are the Son of God."

Reflections

1. Do you believe in Jesus? Do you believe He is the given Messiah? That He was crucified and rose again? That He's coming again?

2. Can you say, from where you stand, that He is your Savior and that His Holy Spirit lives within you? Have you ever consciously, genuinely made Jesus the Lord of your life? Accepted His salvation?

3. If you haven't, will you now? If this is the moment of your salvation, do not take it for granted or let it pass or even weaken. There will always be something trying to convince you to ignore the nudge of the Holy Spirit. But if His grace is calling to you, if you hear the still, small voice within your soul, if you're even just curious about Him, your Creator who knows you and calls you, take the time now to talk with Him. God's hand is extended to you, and that is not my promise; it's His.

There are a few words of belief and acceptance in the prayer below, but I encourage you to turn to the end of this book, where you'll find a simple prayer of confession and an invitation to accept the love of Christ. Don't let this hour pass without being sure of your salvation, without the chance to live it together, fully, with Him.

Prayer

Lord, my words are so inadequate to thank You for the gift of Your Son. Forgive us when we don't see You and for how poorly we have received You. Fill this world, Lord, with rejoicing, to the ends of the earth and echoing with the constant praises of heaven: Unto us a child is born. He is Emmanuel. He is God, with us. Freely given. I add nothing more to my heart's prayer, Lord, than to accept You. I believe You sent Your Son, Jesus, to be the final sacrifice, to bridge the gap of sin that separates us from You. I accept the gift as it was given. I accept You as my Lord, my Savior, who not only sees my heart and forgives my sin, but who walks with me daily, who is my help, my counselor, my comfort. Fill me with a light that shines to say, "Christ has come. Christ is here." Father, may I take Your

gospel, adding nothing, hiding nothing, and hand it to the world, simply:
Christ given, crucified, risen . . . and coming again. Amen.

30

Calvary Is Now

I will not leave you as orphans; I will come to you. Before long, the world will not see me anymore, but you will see me. Because I live, you also will live. (John 14:18-19)

We began this book with Easter, and that's where we end. I don't mean the calendar Easter, but the constant state of it, a bright resurrection morning that never ends, a present, living, risen Lord calling us to come and see. Even when we stand crying, like Mary, unable to see the Truth standing in front of us, He calls us by name as real as He called her then. When she heard her name, she recognized His love and knew it was He. That's where we stand—outside the tomb, prepared to weep, able to be deceived—yet He calls us by name and stands ready to be recognized, known and loved (see John 20:10-16).

I'd purposefully gone outside to dig into the Word for the sake of this writing. As I was reading the Gospels while sitting on the balcony, they suddenly became real—very real. They weren't just real as in "believed and accepted," for the root of David has long been the deep root of my heart. And they weren't real like I was stepping back 2,000 years to personalize a biblical time that we sometimes dramatize so much that we forget it was lived by real people making tough human decisions of faith. The Gospels became real in that they came *forward* 2,000 years.

Rather than me visiting Calvary far in the past, Calvary visited me in the present. A very real man—Jesus, in an electric sense of timelessness—seemed to be sitting nearer than usual to remind me that my present was known millennia prior on the cross and that Calvary is *now*. He reminded me that there is no timeline with the Lord. I was there then (in that He knew me then) and He is here now. This is not a fairy tale; it's not a parable. It's not just an inspirational lifestyle, and it most certainly is not just a religion. It is very real. There is a love existing now, both beside me and on the throne, waiting to be greatly known.

I didn't realize until much later in the evening that all of this had been the exact wording of my prayer that morning. At the time I was concerned by the task of writing about "spiritual truth" for the sake of others. Still feeling much like a child myself and beleaguered by humility, I had gone out onto that balcony to search hard, to be certain I was finding Him rather than pieces of myself. I had asked, "Lord, come to me and be real."

I had meant it less literally than He answered. I could almost see the mannerisms of Christ, there in the seat of sun beside me. His willingness to be literal reminded me to be real and literal with Him, to ask for Him to greater degrees than I was usually inclined to expect and to eagerly await the miracles of revelation. ("Ask and you shall receive, seek and you *shall* find" [see Matthew 7:7]).

There was a time when His disciples could hear His voice, listen to Him pray, clasp His hand, feel their own feet being washed by God, feel heavenly love. Though no longer a literal, physical man, He is still real and present. He still lives. For a moment on that balcony, I realized I had once again reached a milestone of understanding in my life and stopped there. He was trying to remind me there was still more, as we have mentioned in previous pages. There was still a greater reality of Him, a stronger sense, a more permanent image to sit before my eyes in order that I may never see anything but Him first, and the rest *through* Him.

Have you ever stared into a light (not purposefully—and don't try this at home) only to look away and have the shape of that light stuck in your vision, like bright spots and black spots wherever you turn your eyes? Even when you've been typing for prolonged periods, if you look at the blank white spaces on the page, you'll see faint lines of text where there are none. Little black letters are burned into your vision because of a backlit document.

Though no longer a literal, physical man, He is still real and present.

The most prevalent time I noticed this—the occasion when the illustration behind it first hit me—I was sitting on a pale wooden barstool in the pulpit of my church in New York City. We'd stopped a music rehearsal to fix a rough patch, and I'd begun to daydream, staring into the empty sanctuary where huge stage lights framed the edge of the balcony, eight altogether, four on each end. As I was called back to attention, my eyes tried to blink away the spots the lights had burned into my vision—black and white spots, four in a row, a perfect replica of those into which I'd been staring. I laughed at my blindness, and my dear friend Stace, who was standing beside me, said, "There's a devotional in there; write it down." That was years ago, and I just got around to it.

But the image sticks: If you lock eyes with the Light, His image will be before you wherever you turn, overshadowing whatever you face, sometimes blocking what you see and replacing it with a reflection of Him. The longer you've been staring into the Light, the more unshakable these images become. You can change your focus a million times, blink and rub, fight and scratch, try to look in some wrong direction, but the images don't fade until you've been looking away from the Light long enough. Quite appropriately, this phenomenon of light-burned images disappears even faster if you stare into the darkness, cover your eyes and wait for the memory of the Light to fade.

Lock eyes with the Light and He will be before you, securely unshakable, steady and firm. Draw near to Him, and He will draw near to you (see James 4:8). No matter how far you've come and how close you feel, no matter where you stand, ask Him either again or for the first time, but sincerely, to be real to you. Ask where the good road is (see Jeremiah 6:16). Ask Him to grasp your hand and reveal a greater knowledge of Him, whatever the next level of love is. Ask Him for more familiarity, more trust, more of something you can't even identify enough to wish for, but which He knows.

Lock eyes with the Light
and He will be before you, securely
unshakable, steady and firm.

Ask Him, and when you recognize Him, follow Him. When you begin to know the voice of the Shepherd, trust Him. Look for who He is.

He loves you, He loves you, He loves you. When all the other subjects, discussions and issues have been hashed through, the one that rises to the top and remains is that He loves you. It's His own greatest commandment in reverse.

Jesus replied: " 'Love the Lord your God with all your heart
and with all your soul and with all your mind.' This is the
first and greatest commandment. And the second is like it:
'Love your neighbor as yourself.' " (Matthew 22:37-39)

Ever our example, He honors those words as *His* greatest
commandment too. He calls us to first love Him, above all else,
and so He does the same. Above all else, He first loves you (see 1
John 4:19).

Reflections

1. Beyond the worship, praise and personal relationship you
   have with Christ as your Lord and Savior, how much thought
   have you given to His brotherhood? Are you able to step into
   His company as "friend," which He's invited you to do?
2. Giving full weight to an almighty God, how often do you consciously consider Him for the Person He is, standing at your
   side?
3. When you are thinking of the people closest to you—their
   needs, your love for them—do you consider the person of
   the Holy Spirit with as much literal, immediate attention? Is
   there something you can do to pull Him more personally,
   presently into your day and your attentions today?

Prayer

*Jesus, let that be my prayer in every waking moment: "Come and be real to
me." And thank You that You are. Lord, come constantly nearer and simply sit with me. Be all that I don't know how to ask for. Burn the image of
Your character into my eyes and let that be the only light through which I
see the world around me. Whether I'm waiting or feasting, listening or
speaking, walking through the wilderness or into the land of milk and*

honey, I do so with You, Lord. Come to me, sit with me, call to me from the shore to put down my net and walk with You, and I will. Help me to start now, Lord. Whatever today is about to bring, start here with me. Or rather, let me start here with You, wherever You may be and wherever You are going. Keep it constantly on my lips: "Where are You going, Father? Rabbi? Lord? Will You take me with You?" Amen.

Invitation

Someone counseled me before writing this invitation to keep it simple, reminding me of one of the strongest biblical principles: Add nothing to the gospel.

Simply, the God of Abraham, creator of the universe, gave Jesus, His only Son, as the final payment for all sin, so that His Spirit and the doors of heaven would be opened to all His children. He asks us only to accept what He's done for us and take His hand.

Better than any theological explanation I can give you is the testimony of Christ in my own life. As I shared in the introduction, even when I thought I already had God in my life, I was missing the relationship—which was missing everything. I tell you, I never want to go back to the days before Christ became who He is in my life. I never expected to find what He brought or become who He's making me. I never expected the joy I live in still.

If you've never invited Christ to be Lord of your heart and life, don't let this moment pass. He's available, present, waiting and loving you so tremendously. No matter who you are, where you are, what keeps you from Him, there's not a question or obstacle to which Christ is not the complete resolution. Even if you struggle in your belief, hand that to Him and allow Him to come in and build your faith, to "help [your] unbelief" (Mark 9:24). There's no one reading this with whom He isn't present, wanting you to know Him and be safe within His hands.

> This is good, and pleases God our Savior, who wants all men to be saved and to come to a knowledge of the truth. For there is one God and one mediator between God and men, the man Christ Jesus, who gave himself as a ransom for all men—the testimony given in its proper time. (1 Timothy 2:3-6)

There is an immediate need for Him, for the salvation that only He can bring, both for eternity and for this day. Like a specific antidote to a specific poison, there is no substitute for Christ's saving grace in our lives. He knows the spiritual realm and is trying to tell us that it's His name alone that has the power to heal, the power to save, the holiness to love completely and the sovereignty to remain.

> Thomas said to him, "Lord, we don't know where you are going, so how can we know the way?"
>
> Jesus answered, "I am the way and the truth and the life. No one comes to the Father except through me. If you really knew me, you would know my Father as well. From now on, you do know him and have seen him." (John 14:5-7)

I invite you—but more importantly, *He* invites you—to lean into the loving arms of Christ, who's calling, "Come home." An almighty God knows you intimately and calls you now. Christ turns no one away. If you refuse His hand, it's your own rejection, not His.

> For God so loved the world that he gave his one and only Son, that whoever believes in him shall not perish but have eternal life. For God did not send his Son into the world to condemn the world, but to save the world through him. (John 3:16-17)

You don't need any special words. God sees your heart and speaks your language. He will lead you. But this prayer is left here for you, too, to walk you through.

Jesus, I believe in You. I believe that my sin separates me from You, and I don't want to be separated. I want Your peace. I want Your power in my life. I want Your love. I ask You to come into my life in all the ways You promise and offer. I believe that You are the Messiah, that You gave Your life as the payment for my own sin, that You died to save me. I believe that

God gave His only Son in order to bridge the gap between Himself and man, and, God, I believe You see me now, loving me just as You did when You gave Your Son, when You gave me life. I ask You to forgive me for my sin and draw me close to You. Lead me strongly, knowingly, daily in Your way. Direct my life; bring me to life at its fullest through Your Spirit; grant me the eternal life You've prepared. I ask You to come into my life as Savior, friend, Lord. I accept Your invitation. I want to know You. Help me to know You. In Jesus' name, Amen.

If you have accepted Him for the first time just now, I encourage you to contact someone who can be a support to you and help you to grow step-by-step in God's direction. Any local church will take the time to share information with you.

And don't let this invitation be only for those who have never accepted Christ as Savior. Let this be an invitation to anyone at any position in regard to God. Let today bring you more of Him. Ask Him for whatever comes next—the next level of Him— more of His voice and power in your life, a firm sense of peace and hope under any circumstances, a new plateau of strength and joy in the Lord. Ask Him for whatever you haven't seen yet, things you wouldn't even think to ask for but which He knows and longs to bestow.

See it, enjoy it, grasp it: a simple gospel, an unfailing love, a creator with a perfect plan, an amazing glory, a finished grace, one risen Jesus who hands all these things to you. The prayer (the relationship) is an unceasing conversation. Let it begin, and He will make sure it never ends.

If you are interested in having Amy Bartlett speak
or perform at your church, event or conference,
or for more information, please contact:

Amy Bartlett Ministries
info@amybartlett.com
www.amybartlett.com